M000158231

PREACH BETTER

preach better

10 WAYS TO COMMUNICATE
THE GOSPEL MORE EFFECTIVELY

CHRIS MCCURLEY, EDITOR

featuring:

CHRIS MCCURLEY	JAY LOCKHART
KEITH PARKER	JACOB HAWK
STEVE HIGGINBOTHAM	WAYNE ROBERTS
CHUCK MONAN	TREY MORGAN
MICHAEL WHITWORTH	ADAM FAUGHN

© 2015 by Start2Finish Books

All rights reserved. No part of this publication may be reproduced, stored in a retrieval system, or transmitted in any form or by any means without the prior written permission of the author. The only exception is brief quotations in printed reviews.

ISBN-10: 1941972330
ISBN-13: 978-1941972335

Library of Congress Control Number: 2014957471

Published by Start2Finish Books
PO Box 660675 #54705
Dallas, TX 75266-0675
www.start2finish.org

All Scripture quotations are from The Holy Bible, English Standard Version®, copyright © 2001 by Crossway Bibles, a publishing ministry of Good News Publishers. Used by permission. All rights reserved.

Cover Design: Josh Feit, Evangela.com

In memory of

Jimmy Jividen

for helping us all to be better.

contents

foreword

You preach! Or at least you want to. You may preach a lot. You may preach several times a day or once a quarter. You may preach before a packed house, or it may be a small house. You may preach to tens or tens of thousands. Every preacher, regardless of the place or the number, has at least one thing in common—we wish we could be BETTER.

How many Sunday nights have we wished we were better? How often on Friday afternoon have we wished we could be BETTER? We know we'll never be the best preacher in the brotherhood, but we sure wish we could be BETTER. We attend lectureships and seminars—we read books and listen to others— all hoping to learn the secret of being BETTER. We hear "that guy" and think, "If I could just preach like him…" or maybe we just think, "If I could preach BETTER than I do now…"

But it seems no one ever says, "Here is how you do it!" Anyone who stands before a group of people with an open Bible surely feels the urge to be BETTER at communicating God's life-giving Word. The BETTER Conference was born out of that desire. We love our fellow proclaimers, and now it is our prayer that this book will enhance that desire and affect even more lives for Christ.

The BETTER Conference and this book have a singular focus—to provide the tools and information to help you BETTER present the Gospel, to preach BETTER. The goal of both is to focus solely on the craft of preaching.

We are thankful for our good friend, Chris McCurley, for making this book available. We know and love each of the authors who have contributed to this book. If you read their words carefully and work to put them into practice you will be a BETTER preacher.

— Dale & Jeff A. Jenkins
The Jenkins Institute

preachbetter.com

introduction

In the sport of track and field, there is an event known as the high jump. The high jump is a rather simple event, at least in theory. It consists of a horizontal bar resting on two standards in front of a large mat. Competitors stride up to the bar and attempt to thrust themselves over without knocking the bar off of the standards. Each time a jumper clears a certain height, the bar gets raised a little higher. The winner, of course, is the one who clears a height no one else can.

Using a technique known as the Fosbury Flop, some of the more skilled contestants can clear heights above seven feet. A man by the name of Javier Sotomayor is the current record holder in the event. He set the mark in 1993 with a jump of 8 ft. ¼ in. While talent certainly plays a role in the success of a high jumper, one cannot dismiss the hours of training involved. I have been told that, during workouts, competitors are taught to imagine the bar to be much higher in their minds. This mental imagery is meant to assist them in clearing the bar more easily.

As preachers, let us imagine the bar much higher. Let us continually raise the bar in order to enhance our effectiveness and improve our impact. It's okay to fall short. We all fail from time to time. There is no shame in reaching higher and missing the mark. What is a shame is to aim too low.

My aim for this book is simple: to help preachers become better. When we think of being better preachers, we often think of better delivery or better content. Certainly these are important aspects to preaching, but being better is not limited to what occurs in the pulpit. Raising the bar often takes place outside of the pulpit. Aiming higher involves better planning, better study habits, better organization, and a better prayer life. Our effectiveness on Sunday is determined by our efficiency on Monday through Saturday. This does not mean, of course, that certain facets pertaining to content or delivery are unimportant. Better preaching demands a focus on things like using illustrations effectively, applying the lesson, and offering an invitation. In short, raising the bar involves a commitment to excellence in and out of the pulpit.

To help us in our endeavor to preach better, I have solicited the help of nine godly men who are well acquainted with the intricacies of preaching. These men have agreed to provide wise counsel, practical insight, and loving encouragement. This is not a compilation of scholarly essays. This is real-life, real-world information intended to be easily understood and applied. Each chapter is written by a faithful servant who has been in the trenches so to speak. They are writing with one goal in mind: to assist preachers in being better.

I have been told that half way up Mt. Everest, there is a lodge where people can sit and relax and gaze upon the majestic scenery. Many folks like the accommodations so much that they decide not to climb any further. I can't say that I blame them. More than 160 people have died attempting to reach the summit of Mt. Everest, so I perfectly understand why someone would settle for half way. Half way is easier. It requires less sacrifice and commitment. But while half way may be acceptable for someone climbing Mt. Everest, it is certainly not acceptable for someone occupying the pulpit on Sunday.

It is so easy for complacency to set in. It is easy to get satisfied. There is always a desire to kick your feet up and say, "I have made it. That's good enough." To keep climbing is much more difficult and demanding because it requires sacrifice. It requires a total commitment. It requires everything you have got.

Do not be satisfied with half way. Raise the bar. Keep climbing.

Preach better!

— Chris McCurley
Abilene, Texas

1

better planning
chris mccurley

Every day, we eat. We eat because we like the taste of food. We eat to get the proper nourishment and live a healthy life. We eat to give ourselves the energy we need to function. We eat because we are bored, or because we are sad. Whatever the reason, we all eat, and we all eat on a regular basis. There are a lot of things we can put off or skip until a more convenient time, but when it is time to eat, the world stands still. As we consume food, it goes into our bodies and begins to be digested. Through the digestion process, the body keeps what it needs and eliminates what it does not. As a result, much of what we eat actually becomes a part of our bodies. In John 6:35, 48-51, Jesus stated this:

> I am the bread of life; whoever comes to me shall not hunger, and whoever believes in me shall never thirst. … I am the bread of life. Your fathers ate the manna in the wilderness, and they died. This is the bread that comes down from heaven,

> so that one may eat of it and not die. I am the
> living bread that came down from heaven. If
> anyone eats of this bread, he will live forever. And
> the bread that I will give for the life of the world
> is my flesh.

Just as we consume food, we consume Jesus as well. When we eat of his flesh and drink his blood, He becomes a part of our bodies—His thoughts, His words, His character, His way for us. When we eat his flesh and drink his blood (in a figurative sense, of course), we digest all that He is and all that he gives. Christ is life, and we should devour all that He is and that He did so that we are "ate up" with Him. We consume Christ so that He will consume us. When we take Him in, we take Him on. The apostle Paul summed it up perfectly when he wrote: "I have been crucified with Christ. It is no longer I who live, but Christ who lives in me" (Gal. 2:20).

Jesus was encouraging the crowd in John 6 to hunger for something more. Droves of people were following Him, not because they craved spiritual insight, but because they wanted to be fed again. Jesus had just filled their stomachs with a mere five loaves of bread and two fish. To be full in that day and age was extremely rare. Most people teetered between hunger and starvation; therefore, this mob stayed hot on the heels of Jesus in the hope that He would whip up another meal as soon as their stomachs started to growl. Our Lord dashed their hopes and messed with their heads as He informed them that He would no longer cater to their physical appetite. Our Lord bypassed their stomachs and offered the people soul food. By inviting the crowd to eat of His flesh and drink His blood, Jesus was presenting them with eternal sustenance.

Everyone must eat in order to sustain life. Yet, even if we

eat a balanced diet with just the right amount of servings from the dairy group, and so many servings from the meat group, and the proper amount of servings from the bread and cereal group, along with the recommended servings of fruits and vegetables, we can never sustain life indefinitely. If we drink the recommended 64 oz. of water per day, if we do not gulp our water while we eat, and if we do not eat anything after 7:00 p.m. as the experts advise, we may be the picture of health, but we will not live forever. The healthiest person on the planet still has a standing appointment with death. Jesus wanted the crowd to understand that whetting their appetite with the physical things of this world (i.e. bread and fish) was strictly a short-term solution. The true bread that comes from heaven is Christ, and consuming this loaf will not only make one spiritually healthy; it will sustain for all eternity.

the preacher & planning

The preacher wears many hats. He takes on a myriad of roles, but his primary obligation is to offer nourishment, to feed the hungry, to assist people in ingesting and digesting God's word so that they can grow to be healthy, mature Christians. This weekly task is made even more challenging when one considers the diversity of the flock. In every congregation, there are babes in Christ, mature Christians, and varying levels of spiritual maturity in between. Some need milk. Others need meat. The preacher's challenge is to create a menu that will provide sustenance to all.

Sunday comes every week; that is an irrefutable fact. The preacher may be involved in many other activities during the week, but Sunday is the one day that he must plan for above all else. This planning cannot begin on Saturday night. Ideally, it should not begin on the previous Monday either. Proper planning for the preacher is something that should occur weeks, months, or even a year in advance. That is not to say that one cannot be effective by planning week-to-week or even day-to-day, but preachers need to be able to look past the immediate and see the broader scope.

We live in a fast-food culture. We can pull up to a speaker and order our food, drive up to a window, pay for it, and receive it without ever having to leave our car. We can grab a meal out of the freezer, pop it in the microwave, and have supper in a matter of minutes. However, what is easiest and most convenient is not always what is best. A diet consisting only of fast-food leaves one improperly nourished and unhealthy. In preaching, we cannot settle for fast food. Throwing something together on Saturday night can lead to malnourished folks on Sunday morning. The congregation needs a preacher who, like a gourmet chef, spends time in the kitchen, carefully crafting the feast that he will set before them. You cannot microwave a sermon.

Those who preach will attest to the fact that devising a single sermon takes persistent plodding and planning. All preachers have experienced both the stress and the satisfaction at the conclusion of a Sunday spent in ministry. Mentally and emotionally shot, they sink into their recliner or crawl into their bed and reflect on the day's activities. Quickly, they are reminded of the fact that they must repeat the entire process in the coming week. I can recall, as a young preacher in southwest Missouri, being overwhelmed by the demands of ministry. For the first two months of my tenure, I preached my heart out. I was never satisfied with my efforts, but I gave it my all. I worked tirelessly to be the next great preacher in the church. I can vividly remember going home on Sunday evening after a long day and crashing on the couch. I was exhausted, but more than that, I was worried sick. I had preached everything I knew. I had nothing left in the tank. It only took me two months, and I had already run out of material. What was I going to do? How would I survive? Among the many things I needed to learn was a lesson in planning.

Planning is important because preaching is not random. Preaching is not directionless. Preaching should always have a purpose. It should have an aim, a goal. Ministry should be moving, which means we must utilize vision to identify where we are headed. The preacher does not piece together arbitrary and aimless thoughts when constructing a sermon. He does not casually throw something together hours before he is to preach. He does not dare enter the pulpit unprepared. One who does do this has shown himself to be lazy and dishonorable to the task that God has called him to carry out. Preaching is not for the faint of heart. It is grueling and arduous at times; however, the preacher can make his duty even more taxing by not planning properly. A preacher with vision can greatly help his cause. Looking beyond the week-to-week, Sunday-to-Sunday routine can prove to be very beneficial.

creating a menu

Unfortunately, stress and panic can be key virtues in the life of a preacher. A yearly plan can reduce anxiety and function as a GPS to navigate one through the twisting turns of ministry.

Here is what I suggest: Create a menu for the year. This menu should include what you plan to feed the congregation for that year. If you grew up in a home where your mother planned meals for the week, you have an idea of what creating a menu entails. Each week, my wife goes to the grocery store. She does so with a list of the different meals she will be cooking for each day of the week. This allows her to avoid the headache of deciding what to conjure up each evening for our family of five. Planning a spiritual menu works the same way. Look at the year in front of you. Decide what meals you will prepare. By doing this, you will alleviate much of the stress that comes with week-to-week preparation. Preaching is made much easier when you confront Monday already knowing what you will preach on Sunday. This type of planning provides a definite structure and clear-cut direction.

A Balanced Diet

Menu planning begins toward the end of the previous year. Instead of going to the grocery store, go on a retreat. Get away from the office. Where I preach, the staff spends a day or two away from the office each October. We enjoy fun and fellowship with one another as we talk about the year in front of us. We discuss a theme for the coming year. Once we have decided on a theme, we consider Bible Class topics and sermon ideas. We ask two very important questions—what have we done and what do we need? We want to provide the best possible nourishment for our body (the church). This means that we must focus on a well-balanced diet. Some topics are important and may need to be preached on more than once in a year. However, a well-balanced spiritual diet will seek to provide a variety of foods (topics) with the purpose of promoting health and inciting growth.

Different diets must also be taken into consideration. Some church members are babes in Christ; therefore, they are not ready for meat. They still require the milk of God's word.

However, some moved past a liquid diet long ago and require more solid sustenance. In light of the varying spiritual maturity levels in the congregation, it is important to create a menu that satisfies the hunger of the whole. With this in mind, there are 25 topics that I would suggest preaching on every year:

- Attitude
- Authority
- Baptism
- The Bible
- Christ
- Christian Living
- The Church
- Error (Religious & Worldly)
- Evangelism
- Faith
- Forgiveness
- Grace
- Growth
- God
- Heaven
- Hell
- Hope
- Love
- Marriage
- Obstacles to Faith
- Prayer
- Salvation
- Sin
- Stewardship
- Worship

I would suggest creating "recipe files." Dedicate a file to each one of these topics. When you run across an article, an illustration, or any other information pertaining to one of these topics, drop it in the file for future reference when compiling a sermon. This topic list, of course, is not exhaustive. There may be other subjects worth adding. You may prefer to alter the list a bit. The point of this itinerary is to organize and focus the preacher's efforts.

It should be noted that one should permit himself some leeway when creating a menu. Adaptation and flexibility are paramount in preaching. Exercise discretion and make changes if necessary. You may plan a sermon for every Sunday of the year, then an issue arises in the congregation that demands attention from the pulpit. There are times when mitigating circumstances determine a menu change. Many years ago, an elder at the church where I serve went into emergency surgery on Saturday evening. The prognosis was not good. The remaining elders and I stayed at the hospital most of the night. We determined that it would be more appropriate to have a prayer service during worship on Sunday morning in lieu of the usual sermon. This unforeseen circumstance is just one example of how our best-laid plans may need adjusting.

Dietary Needs

Jesus knew precisely what the crowd needed in John 6. They needed Him. They needed spiritual sustenance. The preacher needs to be aware of the dietary needs of the church. Like the crowd in John 6, all people need Jesus, but a spiritual diet consists of various elements necessary to assist one in becoming a faithful follower. That is why another important consideration pertaining to planning is identifying where your congregation's diet is deficient. What are the needs of the body? Are there certain growth areas that need attention? Planning includes an examination of the overall spiritual health of the body. To provide the best possible menu, the preacher, along with the elders, need to have a firm grasp on what is missing from the member's diet. It is easy to fall into the trap of preaching what is comfortable or, for the sake of our analogy, what tastes best. There are some preachers that focus heavily on foundational truths such as baptism. Some may give the majority of their attention to the subject of evangelism. Others may trend toward preaching primarily on denominational error. All of these topics are worthy and need to be approached from the pulpit, just not every Sunday. A primary goal in creating a menu should be to provide variety and balance.

I was once asked to speak at a very small congregation in a rural Texas town. The setting was a Gospel Meeting in which a different local preacher spoke each night. The overall theme focused on worship. My topic was "Why the Church of Christ Does Not Use Instruments." While the theme and topic were certainly deserving of attention, I questioned whether they were appropriate for the venue. This was a church of approximately forty members. All were seventy-plus years of age. I am certain that all of them knew the topic better than I did. I thought to myself, *Why is a church that is struggling to keep its doors open conducting a Gospel Meeting focusing on things that every one of their member's already knows and affirms? How about a theme that targets the lost in the community?* Again, I am certainly not suggesting that the topic of worship is unimportant, or that we should not preach on such a vital subject. I am merely pointing out that some topics are better suited for certain audiences or occasions.

A proper diet is critical to the strength and well being of the church body. When the preacher sets out to create a menu, he is wise to consider the dietary needs of those he preaches to. Not everything he puts on the plate will be tasty. Not every subject he approaches from the pulpit will be desirable. Preaching can be messy. Preaching is not always about pouring syrup in the ears. Sometimes the preacher offers food that does not excite the senses. Like Brussels sprouts, which I loathe, the preacher's offering may not smell good or taste good, but it is necessary to the church's overall health. Some may reject the spiritual food we are offering. Like a little child who manipulates their tongue to push out the food that their mommy is trying to shovel into their mouths, some Christians will refuse the meal we set before them. However, it is not our responsibility to make God's word acceptable. It is our responsibility to make it accessible.

When my son was smaller, he wanted chicken nuggets and French fries for every meal. He was highly opposed to anything green. Fruits and vegetables were his kryptonite. My wife and I did our best to broaden his diet. We encouraged him to eat a wider variety of foods, including apples, bananas, carrots, green beans, etc. It was a constant battle as we sought to expand his culinary scope. It reached the point where we had to deny him dessert until he ate all of his fruits and vegetables. Eventually, he caved and choked down the repulsive items on his plate. It was a means to an end. He did not see the benefit to his health. He only saw the threat of missing out on dessert.

There will likely be some Christians who fail to see the benefit in certain offerings from the pulpit. Topics like marriage, divorce, and remarriage, hit close to home with virtually everyone sitting in the pew, either directly or indirectly. It is a difficult topic for sure, one that is hard to swallow for some, but it cannot be dismissed. Hell is a hot topic that can make one stir in the seat, but we must not avoid it simply because it is uncomfortable. The massive crowd that followed Jesus in John 6 walked away after hearing His sermon. They left a spiritual feast on the table. They were not interested in Jesus' meal plan. We can learn from our Lord's response—He let them leave. He did not alter the message in order to regain His following. He did not chase them down and beg them to reconsider. He allowed them to walk away unfed. We may have to do the same.

My wife typically prepares meals that the family finds tasty and healthy. She does not, however, prepare several meals at one time so that each person can have exactly what he or she wants. There is one meal. That meal is meant to be filling and nourishing. If anyone in the family does not partake of the meal she has prepared, then they do not eat. You eat what is placed before you, or you go hungry. It sounds rather harsh, but she is not about to cater to the whims of every family member.

In the same way, the preacher's task is not to make everyone happy with every meal he serves. His task is to preach the Word. He must be ready in season and out of season to reprove, rebuke, and exhort with great patience (2 Tim. 4:2). His responsibility is to be diligent to present himself as an unashamed worker who accurately handles the word of truth (2 Tim. 2:15). This approach may be met with some resistance. Some will choose not to partake, but the preacher cannot allow the finicky eaters to change the menu. While he should never be unloving in his presentation of the truth, he should also never avoid the truth or sugarcoat the truth for fear of making someone unhappy. When planning your sermons for the year, do not ask, "What do the people *want* to hear?" Rather, ask the question, "What do the people *need* to hear?"

Promoting Good Nutrition

A final consideration when it comes to planning is how

to promote good nutrition among the members. Our goal as preachers is to provide nourishment. With the proper nourishment comes growth. With growth comes the ability to feed oneself. The shepherds, Bible class teachers, and preacher accept responsibility for aiding in the growth of the individual Christian. However, the church member at some point must take ownership of his or her own personal growth. They must become a self-feeder. The member that feasts on God's Word only during worship or Bible class will be malnourished. Church members should not expect perpetual spoon-feeding. There comes a time when all Christians must remove the bib. A part of the preacher's planning should include a strategy for promoting Bible study, prayer, serving, and other spiritual disciplines that encourage growth and maturity.

We are what we eat. When we feed ourselves with a steady diet of God's word, we grow stronger and healthier in our devotion to Him. The preacher can be a vital part of this growth process, not just by the word he speaks, but by the action he inspires.

conclusion

Virtually all companies and organizations have a plan. They have a vision statement, a disaster relief plan; they have procedures for what to do in case of a fire, an earthquake, a tornado—even a terrorist attack! The church needs to have a plan as well. They need to have clear direction and focus. Obviously, the church's primary purpose is to tell the story of salvation to a lost world. The preacher plays an integral role in encouraging and motivating God's people to fulfill this purpose. There is, however, another priority within the Lord's church that coincides with the church's aim—it is spiritual growth. The preacher is vital in stimulating Christians to greater maturity. It is an awesome responsibility indeed—a monumental task—but one that all preachers should relish and revel in. In order to accomplish this godly assignment, we must have an action plan, a strategy for success. Planning is where it all begins.

Set a time in October or November to have a retreat. Get away with staff, elders, other preachers, or just by yourself and spend time planning for the year to come. In your planning consider the following:

- Theme
- Sermon topics
- What does the congregation need?
- What have we done in the past?
- Mark off significant dates or special occasions on the calendar (e.g. Mother's Day, Father's Day, Easter). These are dates that you might want to preach a specific sermon related to the occasion.
- Consider that some topics may need to be approached more than once in a year (e.g. baptism, sin, evangelism).
- Plan a sermon series. A sermon series can make development of lessons somewhat easier.
- Remember to keep a "Recipe List"—articles, illustrations, and other material related to a particular topic. These can be filed under subject headings that you can refer to in sermon preparation.
- Work ahead. If at all possible, have lessons prepared a few weeks in advance. I have known preachers who had lessons prepared six months to a year in advance. It may be hard to get to that

point, but working ahead will pay off big dividends in the stress department.

- Read. The preacher who is constantly reading is constantly expanding his knowledge-base and creativity.
- Study, study, and study some more. Make Bible study a top priority in your personal life and in your planning process.
- Pray! Pray for wisdom. Pray for discernment. Pray for the church. Pray for your efforts. Pray that God will assist you in getting better.

To be better is a resolve that each and every one of us should be committed to. Even the best preacher can be better. Even the best Christian can be better. It is vital that we strive to be the best we can be in order to assist God's children in being the best they can be.

Our world is littered with churches filled with individuals who are being fed cotton candy from the pulpit. It is a message that tastes great, but it has no substance. It is a diet that does not meet the nutritional standards of our heavenly Father and, therefore, is unhealthy. Preachers are responsible for promoting spiritual health. Through better, more strategic planning, we assist the congregation in being well fed and properly nourished.

High in the Alps, there is a monument raised in honor of a faithful guide who perished while ascending a peak to rescue a stranded tourist. Inscribed on the memorial stone are these words: "He died climbing." May the same be said of God's preacher; may we all die climbing!

2

better invitations
keith parker

If I had 100 lives to live, I'd want to live every single one of them as a preacher. If I had 100 sons, I'd want all of them to be preachers. If I had 100 daughters, I'd want all of them to marry preachers. God had only one son, and this one son was a preacher. Being a preacher is not always easy, but preachers make an eternal difference in the lives of people. This is especially seen when preachers offer the invitation of Christ.

Generally speaking, there are three parts to a sermon: the introduction, the body, and the closing (or invitation). The introduction is important because a preacher has about thirty to sixty seconds to capture the attention of his audience. If a preacher loses his audience in his first few words, the whole sermon could be in vain. The body is important because it is the content, the main thing. It is what the sermon is all about. The body of a sermon addresses two questions: 1) What? and 2) So what? The explanation and application. What does the text say and what does this mean for our daily lives? The closing or invitation is important because souls are at stake. What the preacher says at the end of his sermon may determine if someone goes to Heaven or Hell.

When I was a child, my great aunt lived about 200 yards down the street from us. On Sunday mornings, my dad would pick up Aunt Maggie to take her to church. After worship, we would take Aunt Maggie home, and my dad would occasionally invite her to go home with us. We would pull into her driveway, and as she was opening the door to get out, my dad would say, "You ought to go home with us." Aunt Maggie would usually reply, "Naw, I better get out here." Out of politeness, my dad invited her, but I don't ever remember her accepting the invitation. If she had ever said, "OK, I think I will," my dad would have been shocked.

I think sometimes we preachers offer the invitation to sinners like my dad offered the invitation to Aunt Maggie. We do it to be nice. We do it because it is the polite thing to do. We do it to be religiously correct. We do it, not really expecting people to accept, and if sometimes they do, we are a little surprised. The invitation of Christ deserves better than that.

Listen to the Lord's invitation: "Come to me, all who labor and are heavy laden, and I will give you rest. Take my yoke upon you, and learn from me, for I am gentle and lowly in heart, and you will find rest for your souls. For my yoke is easy, and my burden is light" (Matt. 11:28-30). Jesus wants the burdened and weary to come to him. He desires the discouraged and the depressed to cast their cares upon him. He invites lost people to be saved and the backslidden to come home. What a dynamic desire! What a magnificent invitation! The way we offer the Lord's invitation to the world deserves our very best.

*First, we ought to offer the invitation of Christ **prayerfully**.* Jesus said, "The harvest is plentiful, but the laborers are few; therefore pray earnestly to the Lord of the harvest to send out laborers into his harvest" (Matt. 9:37-38). Not only should we pray for more workers, we ought to pray for the work to be blessed. Paul put it in these words: "Brothers, my heart's desire and prayer to God for them is that they may be saved" (Rom. 10:1). The apostles said that they would devote themselves to prayer and preaching (Acts 6:4). God made a precious promise when he said, "If my people who are called by my name humble themselves, and pray and seek my face and turn from their wicked ways, then I will hear from heaven and will forgive their sin and heal their land" (2 Chron. 7:14). In order for our preaching to be most effective, we must couple our preaching with prayer.

Often, when I go somewhere to preach, on the very first day that I'm there, I ask for a favor. I ask those in attendance to pray for somebody who needs to be saved. Or I ask them to pray for a baptized believer who needs a closer walk with Jesus. Praying churches are responding churches. Show me a church that's given to prayer, and I will show you a group that will respond in a positive and public way to Heaven's invitation.

Not long ago, I preached in a revival in West Tennessee. On that Sunday morning, I asked the church to pray fervently for those in Satan's trap. They accepted the request. Would it surprise you if I were to tell you that twelve precious souls were baptized into Christ? Others in the audience responded for prayer. In fact, there were public responses at every service. You see, when God's people pray, great thing happen (Jas. 5:16).

Think about a friend who is lost. Or, think about a family member, a mom or dad, a son or daughter, a brother or sister who needs Jesus. Would you do something for that special person? Stop right now and call that person's name to the God of creation. Ask God for his mercy and grace. Ask God for opportunities to lead that person to Christ. Pray and pray fervently!

*Second, the invitation must be offered **positively***. When people accept the Lord's invitation, it's a time of great rejoicing. When Philip the evangelist preached Jesus in the city of Samaria, men and women were baptized (Acts 8:12). No wonder Luke says that "there was much joy in that city" (Acts 8:8). Later, when Philip preached Jesus to the Ethiopian eunuch, and he was obedient to the gospel, the mood was positive. The eunuch went on his way rejoicing (Acts 8:39). It is not a bad thing when people "walk the aisle." It's a good thing.

Have you ever noticed that people often do what we expect them to do? It's true with parents and children. If parents expect their children to behave, good behavior is often the result. If parents expect their children to disappoint them, they should not be surprised when they get the expected result. What's true with parents and children is also true with preachers and churches. Our churches often respond like we expect them to. If we expect people to respond in a positive way to the gospel of Christ, that optimism can be seen in our sermons, classes, body language, and overall attitude. The audience can tell if you are expecting anything good to happen. They know if your heart is in the invitation or if you are, like others, excited that the sermon is finally over.

So brothers, keep the invitation positive. Expect good things to happen. Emphasize the blessings of gladly receiving the Word (Acts 2:41). Great things will happen.

*Third, the invitation of Christ must be offered **powerfully***. Paul wrote, "I am not ashamed of the gospel, for it is the power of God for salvation to everyone who believes, to the Jew first and also to the Greek" (Rom. 1:16). Likewise, to the Corinthians Paul penned: "Now I would remind you, brothers, of the gospel I preached to you, which you received, in which you stand, and by which you are being saved, if you hold fast to the word I preached to you—unless you believed in vain" (1 Cor. 15:1-2). The power is in the message, not the man. The power is in the gospel, not the gospel preacher. The power is in the teaching, not the technique. In other words, in order for people to be saved, the Word must be preached (2 Tim. 4:2).

It's amazing to me the number of people that "came forward" on the day of Pentecost. When Peter preached, about 3,000 were baptized (Acts 2:41). Amazing! Incredible! How could one sermon produce so many responses? I think the answer to the question is in Acts 2:37: "When they heard this they were cut to the heart." What did they hear? Read the sermon of Acts 2. They heard the prophet Joel and the psalmist David. They heard the ol' Jerusalem gospel. They heard about Jesus—his death, burial, and resurrection. Therefore, we should not be surprised that so many responded to be baptized. Didn't Jesus say, "I, when I am lifted up from the earth, will draw all people to myself" (John 12:32)?

Take a close look at the content of your sermons. When you preach, is God speaking or you? Are your sermons filled with "book, chapter and verse"? Do people hear "a thus saith the Lord"? God promised that his word would not return to him empty, but that it would accomplish what he desires (Isa. 55:11). So, my brothers, preach the word. Let God do his thing.

*Fourth, the invitation of Jesus must be offered **passionately**.* When I was a kid, I attended a little country church about a mile from our house. Preachers would come our way to preach, and there was one in particular that preached with fire, zeal, and determination. He would come every three or four years to preach in a revival for our little church. Often, he would stop the song leader during the invitation song and give another Bible verse or tell another story. With tears in his eyes and urgency in his voice, he would literally beg people to respond. One day, my own mother wanted to know why. She called the preacher aside and asked him why he preached like he did. "Why do you beg people to respond?" my mother asked. "Why do you stop the song leader? Why don't you preach your sermon, offer the invitation, and if people respond, fine. If they don't, that's not your fault." I'll never forget what the preacher did. He asked for my mother's Bible, and he turned in it to 2 Cor. 5:10-11. He read the passage: "For we must all appear before the judgment seat of Christ, so that each one may receive what is due for what he has done in the body, whether good or evil. Therefore, knowing the fear of the Lord, we persuade others." The preacher closed the Bible, looked at my mother and said, "That's why I preach like I do. I know the terror, the fear of the Lord."

You know, for the life of me, I cannot imagine the apostle Paul getting up and making a nice little talk. I can't imagine Paul getting up, putting his hands in his pockets, and casually inviting people to accept Jesus. But with passion, zeal, and emotion, do you know why Paul persuaded people in Athens, Corinth, Philippi, and Thessalonica? Paul answers, "I'll tell you why; I know the fear of God."

I want you to imagine that you're in a burning house. The house is on fire, but you don't know it. You will die in a matter of minutes unless you leave the burning house. How would you want me to tell you of the danger? Would you want me to walk in, put my hands in my pockets, and casually say, "Hey, the house is on fire, you need to consider getting out"? Sometimes we ministers offer the invitation of Christ like that. We do it casually, lightly, and half-heartily. We do it out of habit and custom. We do it because, "That's just the way we close a sermon." But if you're in a burning house, do you know what I would do? I'd become emotional. I would do the best that I could to get your attention. I would scream, shout, and urgently beg you to leave. That's the way we ought to feel about people being lost. That's the way we ought to feel about the fires of Hell. One day, this world in which we live is going to burn up. "But the day of the Lord will come like a thief, and then the heavens will pass away with a roar, and the heavenly bodies will be burned up and dissolved, and the earth and the works that are done on it will be exposed" (2 Pet. 3:10).

So plead with people. Preach passionately and persuasively. Beg people to respond. Realize that you are a dying man preaching to dying people. Isaiah put it in these words: "Cry aloud; do not hold back; lift up your voice like a trumpet; declare to my people their transgression, to the house of Jacob their sins" (Isa. 58:1). Your words might help some poor, lost sinner escape the fires of Hell.

Fifth, the invitation must be offered **persistently**. The invitation of Jesus is not over after the singing of the invitation song. It is open 24/7—seven day a week and 24 hours every day. I have often preached in a revival, sung the invitation song, attended the needs of people who responded, closed the service with prayer, and a few minutes or hours later, baptized others who wanted to make things right with the Lord.

A good example of what I'm talking about is found in Acts 16. You remember the story, don't you? Paul and Silas are in prison. God sends the earthquake. The one in charge of the prison is ready to commit suicide because he thinks he allowed some prisoners to escape. Paul and Silas stop him and explain that they had not escaped but were ready to share the gospel with him. What happened? He and his entire family were baptized sometime after midnight. Some people are like that. They are private in nature. They are not going to go public with their problems. They are shy and timid. They were created that way. It's not that they are ashamed of Jesus or obeying the Lord, they just don't want to call attention to themselves. Remember, Jesus died for these people, too. He tasted death for every man (Heb. 2:9).

The greatest sermons that preachers preach are not preached on Sundays at the church buildings. The greatest sermons that we preach are the lives we live and the example we set. We must walk the talk as we talk the walk. We must practice what we preach and preach what we practice. But when words are involved in the sermons that we preach, our greatest words may come outside of our worship assemblies. Perhaps in private studies with others or in the parking lot after church. Words like, "I'm praying for you." Or, "I have some lessons that I would love to share with you." Or, "As we were singing the invitation song today, you were on my heart." Or, "I love you and would love to see you obey the gospel."

It would be wise if we preachers remembered the words of Paul: "I did not shrink from declaring to you anything that was profitable, and teaching you in public and from house to house," (Acts 20:20). Some people call Acts 20:20 the 20/20 vision of the church. If the church is going to grow, prosper, and spiritually see, we must do as did Paul—teach people publicly and privately. We must offer the Lord's invitation continuously, in church and out of church. His invitation is always open— even at midnight.

Aunt Maggie died about forty years ago. She was invited many times to our house for Sunday lunch. The invitations were offered and rejected. But how were these invitations offered? Not prayerfully. Not positively. Not powerfully. Not passionately. Perhaps persistently, but as a way of being nice. It was a way of ending a conversation. Don't let the invitation of Jesus become "just the way to close a sermon." For heaven's sake—and for the sake of the lost—give it your best.

3

better illustrations
steve higginbotham

As the preacher was walking to the pulpit, I noticed that in his hand, he was carrying an alarm clock; the wind up kind with the bells on top. When he took his place behind the pulpit, he set that alarm clock in a prominent place on the front of the podium where everyone could see it. Then he said the following:

> Prior to tonight's sermon, I asked brother [Jones] to set the alarm on this clock sitting in front of me. I told him to set it for as short or as long a period of time as he wants. Furthermore, I explained to brother [Jones] that I was going to preach until the alarm goes off. Brother [Jones] has set the clock, but I have no idea how long I have before the alarm goes off. But when it does go off, I am going to stop preaching. It doesn't matter if I'm in the middle of a point, a sentence, or a word; I'm stopping. By doing this tonight, I want to reinforce how unexpectedly the return of

Jesus will be. When he returns, he returns. There
will be no time for conclusions, no last minute
arrangements; time will be up!

With his introduction out of the way, this preacher began
preaching, and he and his alarm clock had my rapt attention that
night. I listened as he extended the invitation at the beginning
of his lesson. He did this in case the alarm went off before he
had a chance to tell people what they needed to do to be saved.
I sat on the edge of my seat, wondering how much time he had
left as he preached a sermon on "The Return of Jesus." Then
suddenly, without warning, it happened. The alarm clock rang
out. The suddenness of it startled me! The preacher, true to his
word, abruptly stopped mid-sentence, stepped out of the pulpit,
and the song leader came to the front and led the congregation
in an invitation song.

Although this preacher's sermon was only twelve minutes
long that night, 42 years later, I still vividly remember it. That's
the power of an illustration. This illustration made that twelve-
minute sermon one of the most memorable sermons I have ever
heard in my life.

Through the years, I have heard many good sermons, and I
have also heard some that were, to put it kindly, below average.
As I reflect upon what made some sermons better than others,
I seem to have identified a common thread in both categories.
The better sermons were sermons that employed illustrations,
and the poorer sermons were the ones in which illustrations
were lacking.

This anecdotal finding should come as no surprise when
I consider this finding in light of Jesus' preaching. Have we
not all been taught "Jesus was the Master Teacher"? Surely we
have, and surely he was. But how did Jesus teach? He used

illustrations. He told stories. He employed parables. In fact, Jesus employed parables so frequently that Matthew said, "All these things Jesus said to the crowds in parables; indeed, he said nothing to them without a parable" (Matt. 13:34).

A parable is a story or illustration intended to help a person comprehend what is being said. Simply defined, a parable is "an earthly story with a heavenly meaning." The word *parable* is a compound Greek word consisting of "para," which means "beside," and "bole," which means "to throw." Therefore, a parable is a story or an illustration that is "thrown beside" a truth with a view toward comparison.

When I was in high school, I took geometry. It didn't come easily for me. But my saving grace in that class was that each day, when our teacher would assign our homework problems, he would also take the time to do a "practice problem" on the chalkboard. That practice problem would not be one of the assigned problems in our homework, but it would be *like* my assigned problems. Consequently, these practice problems were of great value to me in helping me solve the real problems in my homework.

That is the function of parables and illustrations. They serve an important role in every sermon by helping the listener grasp and retain the truths being presented.

However, if we can all agree that Jesus was the "Master Teacher," then why don't more preachers preach like him? When a preacher fails to do the work of reading, listening, looking, and imagining in order to create effective illustrations, he isn't preaching like Jesus.

I think preachers are sometimes afraid of being labeled "story-tellers." The assumption is that story-telling is not preaching, but this assumption is discredited by the Lord himself. Stories capture and hold our attention, and Jesus knew this and took full advantage of it.

Sometimes, I wish the people in the pews could see themselves through the eyes of the preacher. You would be amazed at the listener reaction that occurs when a preacher introduces an illustration. The preacher can begin a sentence by saying, "I once knew a man who..." and heads all over the auditorium will pop up. This demonstrates that stories or illustrations help keep listeners engaged in the sermon.

Stories and illustrations can communicate much better than a cold, stand-alone syllogism. Illustrations help us "dress up," or to use biblical verbiage, "adorn the doctrine of God" (Tit. 2:10).

Stories and illustrations also help us to remember what was taught. Not only do they grab our attention; they help us retain the lesson that was being taught. By way of example, can you remember what your preacher preached just last week? Or if you're a preacher, can you even remember what you preached last week? If it doesn't come to you immediately, what thought process will you engage in to remember that lesson? More often than not, a person will remember an illustration that was used and then, from that "hook," will be able to recall the lesson, itself.

Certainly, I am not advocating story-telling in place of Scripture, nor am I advocating story-telling for the sake of story-telling. However, I am advocating that more preachers should learn to be better story-tellers, make better use of illustrations, look more to their surroundings, and create parables just like Jesus did.

I frequently hear debates among preachers as to which form of preaching is best. Are textual sermons better than topical sermons? Are expository sermons better than narrative sermons? I am convinced there's a place for all forms of sermons if whatever form chosen is sprinkled with effective illustrations.

There is so much to commend the form of expository preaching, but how many sermons did Jesus preach in which he broke down, analyzed, and outlined an Old Testament text? Or how many sermons did Jesus preach wherein he picked a topic and sought to tie together a myriad of Old Testament passages on that same topic? What I do know is that Jesus frequently told stories; he used parables and illustrated the truths he wanted to communicate with whatever form (e.g. topical, textual, expository, narrative) he chose to use.

Furthermore, even the best sermon form can be made to be dull and dry without the use of illustrations. As a preacher, the last thing I want to do is preach a dry and dull sermon; the possibility exists that people won't just think I'm dull and dry—they may also conclude that God and what he has to say to us is dull and dry. As a spokesman for God, I cannot be content with presentations that are merely truthful; I must present God's word in such a way that people not only know what is true, but are moved, compelled, and inspired to obey that truth. Illustrations help the preacher accomplish this goal.

The following are several practical suggestions that will assist you in developing better illustrations for your sermons, and thus help make your sermons become more effective, more memorable, and more like the sermons Jesus preached.

1. Do not insert yourself into someone else's illustration.

If you find a good illustration from someone else, use it. But don't insert yourself into the illustration and "pretend" as if the events happened to you personally.

Not long ago, I listened to a man preach a sermon that was one of "my" sermons I had developed from "scratch." The fact that he was using one of "my" sermons didn't bother me at all; after all, my "scratch" sermon was probably "scratched" up by someone else long before me. But what did bother me about this preacher's sermon was that, as he preached it, he used the very illustrations I used in my sermon, and rather than the events happening to me, he told them as if these events actually happened to him!

To take someone else's experiences and deceive people into thinking those experiences happened to you is simply dishonest and lacking integrity. Furthermore, it makes one wonder about the speaker's motive. Why would he insert himself in an event that didn't really happen to him? If the answer is to cause people to respect him more, or sympathize with him more, then that preacher has lost the purpose of the illustration in the first place. An illustration should not be about the speaker, but about Jesus. If the preacher—rather than Jesus—is being magnified by the illustration, the preacher has lost his way.

If an illustration is a good illustration, it will be just as effective (and not to mention, truthful) if the preacher would simply say, "I know someone who..." Standing behind the pulpit doesn't give a preacher a free pass on lying.

2. Check the truthfulness or accuracy of your illustration.

A preacher immediately loses credibility when he tries to pawn off an "urban legend" as though it really happened. I have heard preachers go into great detail about the meaning of the "folded napkin" that was left in the empty tomb of Jesus. We are told that whenever a master was finished eating, he would crumple his napkin, throw it on the table, and his servant would then know he could clean up his plate. However, if the master folded his napkin and left his plate, the servant would see the folded napkin and know that the master was returning. Therefore, we are told the folded napkin found in Jesus' empty tomb was a message declaring he was coming back. The "folded napkin" is a great story; its only flaw is that it just isn't true. There was no such custom among the Jews. It is merely a fictional story that someone created in his fertile imagination, but it is not rooted in truth.

Not long ago, I heard a preacher inform the congregation that NASA scientists had found a "missing day" that corresponds to "Joshua's long day" in which the sun stood still. Again, there just isn't any truth in that.

Preacher, do your research. Your credibility is at stake. How can you preach to congregations and encourage them to be diligent and studious like the Bereans (Acts 17:11) while you behave like the Thessalonians? If, as a preacher, I don't have my credibility, then what do I have?

3. Don't use illustrations your listeners may not understand.

If you want to make an illustration based on a sticking butterfly flap in an old carburetor, you will probably lose most people because they're unfamiliar with butterfly flaps in old carburetors. It's not that it is a bad illustration; it may just be that it's used on the wrong listeners.

Personally, I am a lover of all things sports. Therefore, many of my illustrations come from sporting events and stories. Not long ago, I used an illustration about a high school football coach in Little Rock, Arkansas whose philosophy is never to punt the ball. This same coach always attempts "onside kickoffs," rather than typical kickoffs. The point I wanted to make by using this illustration was that when we stand against conventional wisdom, we may sometimes find it difficult to stand alone, but if we're right, we need to be courageous enough, even if it means we must stand alone. This coach has received his share of criticism for failing to fall in line with conventional wisdom, but he has found a successful formula that has enabled him to win four state championships. I thought it was a great illustration until I got in the car. On the drive home, my wife, being the kind and gentle lady she is, said concerning my illustration, "I had absolutely no idea what you were talking about tonight." Ouch!

Preachers, make sure your illustrations will be understood by your listeners. Butterfly flaps and onside kickoffs just might be too technical to be understood by many listeners. Remember, illustrations are only effective if they are understood.

4. Don't use an illustration that will probably offend a listener's sensitivities.

Several years ago, a preacher was trying to illustrate the truthfulness contained in Psa. 139:14, "I praise you, for I am fearfully and wonderfully made." Unfortunately, instead of talking about the complexity of the eye, the human skin, or the human respiratory system, he chose to go into detail explaining the complex functions and physiology of the human reproductive system. Had he been lecturing in a medical school, he would have been fine. But he was speaking to a mixed assembly, both in gender as well as age, and his illustration was inappropriate and offensive to many. Always remember the make-up of your listeners. Be sensitive to gender differences, age differences, employment differences, educational differences, as well as racial and nationality differences.

5. Use illustrations from the Bible.

The Bible is one of the best resources for good illustrations.

There are countless stories in the Bible that illustrate biblical truths that challenge us today. Do you want to impress upon your listeners the need for vigilance in not being deceived or led astray? Tell the story of the old and young prophets (1 Kings 13). Do you want to impress upon your listeners how evil companions can corrupt good morals? Tell them what happened to the apostle Peter when he was influenced by his "Judaizing friends" (Gal. 2). Do you want to impress upon your listeners how partial obedience is really just disobedience? What better illustration is there than Saul's disobedience with reference to utterly destroying the Amalekites (1 Sam. 15)?

Isn't this exactly what the apostle Paul did in 1 Cor. 10? He recalled Old Testament events in the history of Israel in order to illustrate the perils and judgment that awaited those in Paul's day who rebelled against God.

6. Use relevant illustrations from timely sources.

Local news, national news, world news, sports, medicine, television, technology, and children are great sources for sermon illustrations. We simply need to open our eyes. We need to train ourselves to see things differently than most people see them.

For example, when a man accidentally falls to his death while reaching for a baseball tossed to him by an outfielder, the world sees a tragedy. But the preacher with vision sees a spiritual lesson on "the unintended consequences of our actions." When the world sees Don Knotts, they see Deputy Barney Fife. However, the preacher with vision sees a spiritual lesson about "type-casting," and how a Christian's life should be so connected to the character of Jesus that, when a person sees us, he can't help but see Jesus. When a little baby girl smiles at her parents for the first time, the world thinks, "How precious."

When the preacher with spiritual vision sees that same event, he sees the joy God must experience when his children respond favorably to him.

Do you see the point? We need to improve our vision. We need to see beyond what the average person sees. We need to train our eyes and ears to pick up on glimpses of God in every aspect of daily life. We need to see what others don't see. When you open your "spiritual eyes," you will find helpful illustrations in nearly everything.

In fact, practice developing your "spiritual sight." Begin watching the news with a pen and pad and deliberately search for spiritual applications. Begin scanning the headlines in the newspaper or on the Internet, not with the intent of simply being current, but for the purpose of finding good illustrations that will help you point people to Jesus.

For me, one of the greatest aids in developing illustrations is keeping a notebook with me. I love technology and have all the latest gadgets, but I have found no more convenient tool to keep track of ideas than a pen and a notebook. My notebooks are prized possessions. They contain seed thoughts, skeleton outlines, and sermon illustrations, many of which have not yet been used.

7. Use illustrations to create suspense, mystery, or tension.

The late radio broadcaster Paul Harvey excelled at this through his weekly segments entitled "The Rest of the Story." Harvey would weave a story with unknown facts about an event or person who was very well known, causing his listeners to be wondering and guessing what or who he was talking about. Finally, at the right moment, Harvey would reveal the mystery, defuse the suspense, and bring resolution by saying, "…and now you know the rest of the story."

Such illustrations require hard work and research, but their reward is the rapt attention of your listeners. Recently, one of the men in the congregation where I preach gave a devotional lesson on a Wednesday night following Bible class. Since it was December, he referenced the classic Christmas movie, *It's a Wonderful Life*. He briefly reminded us of the plot, shared with us how he used to watch the movie every year, shared a few famous lines that jogged our memories, and had us all feeling nostalgic. Then he abruptly informed us that there was one scene in the movie that has caused him to no longer watch the movie. At this point, he had me! I was in suspense as I wondered what that reason might be. He then used that suspense and mystery to take me where he wanted to lead me. It was a great illustration that made a great point, and the mystery and suspense were crucial elements of his illustration.

8. Use obscure Bible characters to illustrate various points.

The Bible contains many characters and events we have simply skimmed over. These characters and events can prove to be useful as illustrations.

For example, consider Eliam. Eliam is one of those obscure Bible characters. More than likely, you don't remember Eliam, but the Bible does record a story associated with him and his daughter. Eliam and his wife had a little girl. That girl grew up, and when she was old enough to be married, Eliam gave her hand in marriage to a man who loved her. However, the lives of Eliam's daughter and son-in-law changed forever sometime after they were married. One day, when Eliam's son-in-law was away, some men came to Eliam's daughter's home, took her, and gave her to their master who abused her. Eliam's son-in-law was unaware of what happened to his wife, and before he could do anything about it, they murdered him. One can only imagine the anger Eliam must have had toward the man who did this to his daughter and his son-in-law. And to think, the man who did this to his daughter was a man, who the Bible says, was "a man after God's own heart..." and now you know the rest of the story.

Did it take a little while for you to figure out who I was talking about in this illustration? Were you wondering why you couldn't remember that story, then at some point did you come to the awareness that I was talking about David and Bathsheba? All I did was tell the story through another man's eyes—Bathsheba's father—and that angle brought freshness to the story. By looking over the shoulder or through the eyes of a bit player in a biblical story, we may find fresh insights into old, familiar stories.

New angles through the eyes of obscure characters can bring a depth to a story or an angle never before considered in connection to that story. The story of Eliam helps us understand the challenge of forgiveness. You see, I have no problem forgiving David for what he did. He's one of my Bible heroes. He was a man after God's own heart. I don't struggle with forgiving him, but do you think Eliam might have struggled? It illustrates the adage, "It's easy to love your enemies until you really have one." Because I told the story of David and Bathsheba through the eyes of another man, I was able to approach that story in a way that I have never done before.

Be creative and develop your own illustrations. Not every illustration has to come from "real-life" situations. Some of the best illustrations were created specifically to teach a lesson. This is precisely what Jesus' parables were. Was there really a man that Jesus had in mind who was beaten and left for dead on the road to Jericho, or did Jesus "create" that story to illustrate the truth he was wishing to convey? Was there really a man who had two sons, one of whom requested his inheritance before his father's death, or did Jesus create that story to teach the truth about the love of God?

Not all parables happened 2,000 years ago. There are countless parables waiting to be written. Some parables aren't rooted in actual historical events, but in the sanctified imagination of preachers who are seeking ways to communicate important truths about God and his will for our lives.

Preacher, learn to be a better story-teller. Work harder on developing relevant, engaging, and captivating illustrations that point people to Jesus. Don't be dissuaded from using illustrations because of a notion held by a minority of brethren that preaching and story-telling are incompatible. Just remember, Jesus was the "Master Teacher," and he was a story-teller (Matt. 13:34).

4

better relevance
chuck monan

You ask me what it means to be irrelevant? The feeling is akin to visiting your old house as a wandering ghost with unfinished business. Imagine going back: the structure is familiar, but the door is now metal instead of wood, the walls have been painted a garish pink, the easy chair you loved so much is gone. Your office is now the family room and your beloved bookcases have been replaced by a brand-new television set. This is your house, and it is not. And you are no longer relevant to this house, to its walls and doors and floors; you are not seen.
— Azar Nafisi, *Reading Lolita in Tehran*

Culture is merciless in eliminating things it deems irrelevant. You don't think so? How many folks do you know these days who drive an Oldsmobile? Watch movies on Beta or VHS tapes? Listen to music on 8-tracks or cassettes? You youngsters might have to Google these to know what they are/were. Even such innovations as the Blackberry have been decimated by the rise of the superior Smart Phone. If you are not seen as relevant, you won't survive.

Churches are not exempt from this dynamic. Examples abound all over the world.

England was once one of the most Christianized nations on earth. In the latter half of the 19th century, more than 75% of English children were regular attendees in Sunday school. But things have changed. From 1968-1999, attendance in the Church of England, already at historically low levels, almost halved from 3.5% to 1.9%. If current trends continue, Sunday attendance could fall to a mere 87,000 by 2050—in a country with a population of 52 million. Last year in England the most popular name for baby boys was *Muhammad*.

George Carey, former Archbishop of Canterbury, says of his church: "I see it as an elderly lady, who mutters away to herself in a corner, ignored most of the time."

So what does this have to do with us? Well, while we can say that Churches of Christ aren't as bad off as the Church of England, how many generations does it take for such a sea change to occur? Only one, friends.

I believe the words of Dan. 2:44 which promise, "In the days of those kings the God of heaven will set up a kingdom that shall never be destroyed, nor shall the kingdom be left to another people. It shall break in pieces all these kingdoms and bring them to an end, and it shall stand forever." The survival of the Lord's church is assured whether we do our job or not. It is Christ's church.

But whether it survives as a remnant or as a flourishing tree that emerges from a mustard seed depends in some measure on us. And by "us," I am referring to our preachers, teachers, and elders. Preachers especially.

Those of us who stand before the congregation every Sunday largely determine whether the church will be seen as relevant or irrelevant. Western culture has already deemed Christianity as passé; if those in the pews agree with this assessment, we are in deep trouble.

But this battle has not been lost. It just requires a different approach for a new time.

A well-known critic of Churches of Christ recently said on Twitter: "Time for Fox's annual War on Christmas report: Chastening those who take Christ out of Christmas. Or as I call it, the church of my youth."

What is interesting about his tweet is not that it is yet another well-aimed barb from him at the church, but that it unwillingly glosses over the fact that most Churches of Christ in his youth had nothing to do with Christmas. Then, Christmas was largely embraced; now, is is used to fire salvos at an increasingly godless culture.

What both of these positions have in common is they take an Us vs. Them attitude. Both squander a golden opportunity to teach and model the meaning of God coming to Earth. When we are either a) antagonistic to other believers, or b) antagonistic to unbelievers, their takeaway about us is the same: these folks are hostile toward and disapproving of, well, everyone.

There is a better way.

Instead of preaching that is reactive, we need preaching that is proactive. Not the Proactive of the acne medication, but creating or controlling a situation by causing something to happen, rather than responding to it after it has happened. Too often, we have defined our Christianity by the sum total of the things we are against and don't do. People aren't particularly interested in what we are against; they prefer to know what we're for. Paul's advice here is helpful:

> As surely as God is faithful, our word to you has not been Yes and No. For the Son of God, Jesus Christ, whom we proclaimed among you, Silvanus and Timothy and I, was not Yes and No, but in him it is always Yes. For all the promises of God find their Yes in him. That is why it is through him that we utter our Amen to God for his glory.
>
> 2 Cor. 1:18-20

So then, the beginning point of relevant preaching is knowing what we're for, not just those things we're against.

what to preach & how to preach it

No one who stands before the church ever feels completely adequate for the job of preaching, or in determining just what to preach. Helpful is Paul's statement to the Ephesian elders, "I did not shrink from declaring to you the whole counsel of God" (Acts 20:27). We cannot preach only those things people are interested in hearing. The whole will of God, or entire counsel of God, includes the bad news of sin, the good news of salvation, and everything in between.

Our preaching must address the deepest needs of mankind. God, Jesus, life, death, sin, forgiveness, grace, despair, hope—who could possibly exhaust these subjects? An example of preaching on such themes in a culturally relevant way is seen in Paul's trip to Athens (Acts 17:16-34).

Tertullian asked the question "What has Athens to do with Jerusalem?" In other words, what does secular culture have to do with Christian culture? In his visit to the intellectual center of the world, Paul answers this question. In so doing, he leaves some important lessons for us to reach and transform our culture:

1. Know the Zeitgeist

Zeitgeist literally translates "the spirit of the times" or "the spirit of the age." Zeitgeist is the general cultural, intellectual, ethical, spiritual climate of a nation or group. It is the general ambiance, morals, sociocultural direction or mood of an era.

Paul understood the zeitgeist of Athens. He knew the language. He knew the schools of philosophy like the Epicureans, Stoics, and Cynics. He was familiar with the religion. He knew the prevailing morality, or lack thereof. He was not a missionary traveling to a place he knew nothing about, unable to speak to the people in their own language.

Centuries before Paul visited Athens, a philosopher named Diogenes lived there. He was bitterly critical of Athenian society, walking the streets during the day holding a lantern, claiming to be looking for an honest man. He said of himself: "I am a citizen of the world." It is easy to see such a spirit in the apostle Paul.

2. Give a compliment

Seeing Athens filled with idols filled Paul with revulsion. So what does he do? Start beating them over the head with Bible verses like, "You shall have no other gods before me," or "You shall not make for yourself an idol," or "An idol is nothing at all in the world?" (Exod. 20:3, 4; 1 Cor. 8:4).

No. He compliments them.

> Men of Athens, I perceive that in every way you are very religious. For as I passed along and observed the objects of your worship, I found also an altar with this inscription, "To the unknown god." What therefore you worship as unknown,

this I proclaim to you.

Acts 17:22-23

In our interaction with others, can we find something good about them to praise? Or do we immediately begin with error and points of disagreement? Too often, Christians are perceived by unbelievers to be against everything. Are we for anything? Let's begin there.

3. Know God

Paul could tell those people about God because he knew God. How can you describe someone you don't know? How can you explain something you know little or nothing about? Paul tells them that God doesn't need a house to keep the rain off his head, nor does he need anything to eat for dinner. He made it all, and it all belongs to him. He is in charge and wants us to seek him.

> Thus says the LORD: "Let not the wise man boast in his wisdom, let not the mighty man boast in his might, let not the rich man boast in his riches, but let him who boasts boast in this, that he understands and knows me, that I am the LORD who practices steadfast love, justice, and righteousness in the earth. For in these things I delight, declares the LORD."
>
> Jer. 9:23-24

4. Speak the language

Paul could reach the Athenians because he was bilingual. By this, I don't mean he spoke both Hebrews and Greek, which he did. He was bilingual in that he not only understood the

Jewish world; he also understood the Greek world. Notice how he models this:

> For in him we live and move and have our being.
>
> — Epimenides

> We are his offspring.
>
> — Aratus

Some Christians think these words are Paul's. They aren't. Paul is quoting these immensely popular Greek poets, who were the ancient equivalent of rock stars. Paul didn't just know the Bible; he knew literature, poetry, art. I have no doubt that if he were alive today, Paul would know the work of Bob Dylan, Bono, and other cultural avatars.

Think of the instant connection Paul gained with his audience by quoting their own cultural giants. It is reminiscent of June 29, 1990 at Tiger Stadium in Detroit as Nelson Mandela began his speech before 50,000 with these words:

> Mother, mother
> There's too many of you crying
> Brother, brother, brother
> These's far too many of you dying

It was like an electric shock as the packed stadium roared its solidarity with the man who had conquered hate... and who knew the words of their own poets.

5. *Tell the truth*

> Being then God's offspring, we ought not to think
> that the divine being is like gold or silver or stone,

> an image formed by the art and imagination of man. The times of ignorance God overlooked, but now he commands all people everywhere to repent, because he has fixed a day on which he will judge the world in righteousness by a man whom he has appointed; and of this he has given assurance to all by raising him from the dead.
>
> Acts 17:29-31

God had not judged them for worshipping false gods in their ignorance, but time is running out. Now he commends all people everywhere to repent. The resurrection of Jesus from the dead is proof that God is in control.

When they heard about the resurrection of the dead, some of them sneered. Some still sneer today. But some will believe.

> If Jesus rose from the dead, then you have to accept all that he said; if he didn't rise from the dead, then why worry about any of what he said? The issue on which everything hangs is not whether or not you like his teaching but whether or not he rose from the dead.
>
> — Timothy Keller

Qoheleth (or The Preacher) opined, "There is nothing new under the sun..." (Eccl. 1:9). The same questions men and women have today are the questions that have concerned mankind for millennia. Preach those questions and God's answers to them.

A current temptation for preachers these days is to avoid preaching Christian doctrine. Many today, in the church and out of it, have concluded that doctrine isn't important. We've all likely heard armchair theologians opine, "Well, that isn't a salvation issue..." I'm more than a bit leery determining what does and doesn't matter to the Lord. Paul reminds the young preacher Timothy, "Guard your life and doctrine closely" (1 Tim. 4:16). Do you think if doctrine were of minor or no importance that the Bible would issue such a warning?

Four decades of preaching has helped me understand that balance is key. (As Jay Lockhart deals with this in another chapter, I encourage you to read his excellent advice on this matter). Avoiding biblical teaching on salvation, worship, the church, and other vital issues is a sure way to produce biblically illiterate Christians. People want to know what the Bible says about our practices. To assume everyone already knows is to assume too much. As if a reminder were necessary, a recent sermon I preached on why we sing *a cappella* resulted in more requests for the sermon tape/DVD than any in recent memory. Do not neglect basic, fundamental, doctrinal lessons. Otherwise, we will raise up a generation that "knew not Joseph."

This is particularly true for baptism. Churches of Christ have long been known for insisting on the necessity of baptism in obeying the Gospel. It has always been so and always will be. This requires diligence as we call our listeners to obey Christ. A Baptist minister, J.D. Greear, raised eyebrows recently with his book *Stop Asking Jesus Into Your Heart.* Admitting that the "Sinner's Prayer" is found nowhere in the Bible, he encourages a different approach to calling people to conversion. It is encouraging to see others recognize that the difference between baptism and the mourner's bench is that "one is from heaven, and the other from the sawmill," in the words of "Raccoon" John Smith.

Another emphasis for preachers today must be apologetics. It is embarrassingly tragic that Christians have allowed skeptics to use science as a cudgel to batter believers. All truth belongs to God, and as Dr. Frances Collins says, DNA is "the language of God." If the apostle Paul had access to the vast body of scientific knowledge we have, he would've used it to create faith in and bring glory to God. As more young adults drift away from faith in God, we must use the classroom, pulpit, and coffee shop to teach that faith in the Creator is not only reasonable but indispensable.

how to stay relevant

When I started preaching in 1987, some unsolicited advice came from my father-in-law. Since he had been preaching since around the time of World War II in a career that included turns as a college professor, dean, administrator, minister, elder, and author, attention must be paid. His message?

"If you quit studying, you're dead."

He was right.

"Do your best to present yourself to God as one approved, a worker who has no need to be ashamed, rightly handling the word of truth" (2 Tim. 2:15). Of paramount importance here is our knowledge and treatment of Scripture. But of secondary importance is our study and awareness of a broad range of knowledge. The apostle Paul's familiarity with the Gentile world and their poets earned him a hearing in Athens (Acts 17:16-34).

The old English word *parson* literally meant "the person." He was called this as, by his person, the church was represented, but also because he was the person to whom you would go for answers. In a time where fewer are coming to us for answers, it is crucial that we study to show ourselves approved.

John Buchanan, editor/publisher of *The Christian Century*, writes, "Reading is the necessary backdrop to relevant 21st-century preaching. There is no shortcut or substitute. When the gospel and the preacher's personal faith and experience are informed by wide, disciplined, varied, and sustained reading, lively and compelling sermons will be the result."

Karl Barth advised preachers to work up their sermons with a newspaper in one hand and a Bible in the other, but to interpret the newspaper with the Bible. The minister must be a student of culture, able to understand the times, as did the men of Issachar (1 Chron. 12:32).

> Preaching is compelling to young secular adults not if preachers use video clips from their favorite movies and dress informally and sound sophisticated, but if the preachers understand their hearts and culture so well that listeners feel the force of the sermon's reasoning, even if in the end they don't agree with it.
>
> — Timothy Keller

I can usually tell within minutes how rigorous a minister has been in study. Bland, generalized religious clichés take center stage in the sermon. I nearly fell over laughing recently in reading the quirky and irrelevant Anne Lamott's gripe, "People are always saying, 'Let go and let God...' and I just want to stab them."

More sympathetic I could not be.

Lazy, non-existent reading habits also result in dependence on the Internet, published sermons, and stories pulled from books containing nothing but familiar illustrations. Everyone uses these from time to time, but don't make a habit of them. The best supporting material comes from digging up your own stuff, as Alvin Plantinga, Jr. notes:

> ... reading general literature just for illustrations is slightly perverse. I want to read for better reasons

and especially to be deepened and expanded by
my reading. Reading gives me more substance to
bring to Christian life and to Christian preaching.
The thoughtful preacher gets a little bigger each
time she reads. But, yes, along the way she will
also discover a story, an incident, a saying that is
striking enough to belong in a future sermon.

His use of the feminine pronoun notwithstanding, Plantinga
makes a good point.

Such an experience happened to me a couple of years ago.
Reading Ron Powers' magisterical biography of Mark Twain
uncovered an encounter the American literary icon had with
Alexander Campbell. The famed reformer Campbell came
to Hannibal, Missouri, and preached a sermon on the town
square. Young Sam Clemens marveled at the turnout: "That
was the first time in my life that I had realized what a mighty
population this planet contains when you get them all together."
Campbell's audience wanted printed copies of the sermon, and
the newspaper shop where Clemens worked printed 500 copies
for $16, a huge amount of money in a time when Hannibalians
usually settled debts with sugar, coffee, turnips and onions.

Clemens' fellow employee was the seventeen-year-old
Wales McCormick. Clemens described his amoral friend as "a
reckless, hilarious, admirable creature; he had no principles,
and was delightful company." As the shop worked on Campbell's
order, Clemens and his dim pal had an encounter with the
illustrious theologian:

This visit produced what might be called the
Gospel according to Wales. In one version of the
story, Twain insisted that when Campbell stopped
by Ament's shop with the sermon, he overheard

McCormick exclaim, "Great God!" The preacher took the boy aside and admonished him that "Great God!" was blasphemy, and that "Great Scott!" would be one example of an acceptable substitute. McCormick apparently took this to heart: while correcting the proof sheet of the sermon, he dutifully changed Campbell's own pious use of "Great God" to "Great Scott." Taken with the spirit, he amended "Father, Son & Holy Ghost" to "Father, Son & Caesar's Ghost," and then improved even that bit of euphemism – to "Father, Son & Co."

Wales's moment of divine reckoning approached when he removed the full name "Jesus Christ" from a line in the sermon to create more space, and substituted "J.C." For some reason, this infuriated Campbell as he read the proof sheet; he strode back to the print shop and commanded McCormick: "So long as you live, don't you ever diminish the Savior's name again. Put it all in." McCormick took this advice to heart: the revised line came out, "Jesus H. Christ."

— Ron Powers, *Mark Twain: A Life*

You won't find things like this on sermonillustations.com. You have to dig for it yourself.

This story reminds that people have always been profane, ignorant, and generally clueless about the sacred. It serves to help us avoid the pitfall of giving into romanticizing the past by assuming there was a time when America was a "Christian nation." As the Bible counsels, "Say not, 'Why were the former days better than these?' For it is not from wisdom that you ask this'" (Eccl. 7:10). And it's interesting to know that Alexander Campbell and Mark Twain crossed paths.

If your mind stays sharp and active, it will show in your preaching.

Another way to stay relevant is to get out of the office and spend time among non-Christians. Too often, we've become too busy inside the church to know those outside the church. As a result, we don't hear what they think about life, church, spirituality, and Christians. We aren't able to build relationships with those we don't take the time to get to know.

In his book *They Like Jesus But Not the Church*, Dan Kimball recounts speaking to a gathering of preachers about spending time at the coffeehouse, engaging in conversations with non-Christians. As he spoke there were puzzled looks on the faces of the ministers. He writes:

> Finally someone raised his hand and asked if the leaders and people of my church allow me to do this instead of spending time with the people in the church. Someone commented that they couldn't possibly go to a coffeehouse like that, since their church expects them to be available in the church office during the week to care for the "flock" (his word).
>
> This caught me off-guard, so I asked if others felt the same way, and to my surprise many of them did. They felt their job as church leaders is to preach the Scriptures and stay in the church office all week long to be available for the people of the church. One person commented that non-Christians need to come to the church building and that revival meetings and "altar calls" are the way to reach them. Many indicated that it isn't church leaders' job to go out to the people; instead the people should come to us. Another commented about how "pagan" emerging

generations are and how they just need to hear solid preaching, which will cause them to repent of their ways.

How many times do the Gospels record Jesus interacting with regular people? How many times does he accept a dinner invitation or go to a wedding? Ask a woman for a drink? Invite himself to a tax collector's house? He was involved in people's lives. How relevant will we be—will our preaching be—if we only associate with those just like us?

go forth & announce the gospel

The work you do as a spokesman for God is more important than we can possibly understand. Ours is a message that will always be relevant. I recall hearing Jimmy Allen say that he cringed whenever he heard someone say we need to make the Bible relevant. The Bible is relevant, he reminded. It's those of us who preach it who veer from time to time into irrelevance. Devote yourself to preaching this relevant message in a relevant way.

The crowd may not notice the ways in which the pulpit lends you gravitas, as though you stand in front of the sturdy furniture of God's own mind, but the benefit is still yours. As a soldier salutes the rank before the officer has earned a salute, so a congregation may attend to the one behind the pulpit, even if his words fall among them haphazardly.

That podium is a bulwark, evoking in its angles and height the church that guards the deposit entrusted to it. More basically, however, the pulpit evokes the logos itself: the foundation for thought, life, and being; a principle of order that bestows itself here; a single, unmoving point in a tilting universe.

This may be part of why I favor the simple pulpit to the ornate: clean lines and darkness bring to mind an Archimedean geometry that is invoked as the Word disseminates into the cosmos. The servant of God extrapolates these living truths from behind his podium, praying for a single bored face to turn. When the words catch and a single congregant nods in sudden assent, the pulpit becomes a fixed outcrop for a hand to grasp in a thundering crush of time against eternity. History rushes and breaks upon this book; centuries of strife and wonder crack into halves over it.

The book still sits; the pulpit still stands. The preacher finds his words, and from the pulpit, those words go out again.

— Martyn Wendell Jones

5

better passion
michael whitworth

I watch a lot of football. Every year in late August, the anticipation of another season makes me so excited that I can barely stand it. I love the pageantry of college football. I love the skill and talent of pro football. I've been watching the sport border-line religiously nearly all my life. And though I've never played or coached football, I know what a football player must possess to be successful.

A lot of skills related to one position or another can be taught or coached. If a player has poor pass-blocking skills or can't tackle well, a coach can often correct that if the player is willing to learn and train himself under the coach's instruction. The mental X's and O's can also be taught to most any player willing to apply himself. But there's one thing coaches can't teach, and athletes can't learn. You either have "it" or you don't.

Speed.

Coaches can't coach speed, and athletes can't learn it. Sure, they can exercise and lift weights. They can run sprints and do resistance training. But most any football insider will tell you that speed on the field is something that can't be taught. A player is born fast, or he's not, and that's about it.

I think what speed is to football, passion is to preaching. I may be way off here, but it seems that passion in a man's preaching may be the irreplaceable "x-factor" that you either have, or you don't. Someone can teach you how to illustrate a sermon, how to offer a better invitation, or how to be more relevant. But teaching passion? My fear is that passion that can be "taught" might come across as fake or forced.

I offer that semi-disclaimer so that you won't expect me to work miracles as I go through this chapter. I can't teach you passion, nor am I the person qualified to kindle it within you.

But I know Who can!

Before we start, let's make sure we're on the same page when it comes to passion. I'm not talking about a hyperactive performance in the pulpit that makes the entire worship service seem like a slightly-subdued circus. I doubt that God is honored and lives are changed long-term by a lot of dramatic whooping and hollering.

I'm not talking about temporary, use-once-then-discard passion. All of us have been temporarily inspired by a movie or book or life-event. I preached very passionately after my son was born and after I saw the movie *Remember the Titans*. Also, when I was younger, a can of Mountain Dew or Red Bull would help me preach passionately. But these methods of injecting passion into our preaching are false and short-lived.

I also concede that's one passion in the pulpit is mitigated or supplemented somewhat by one's personality. An extroverted preacher will find it easier to bring pep to the pulpit; an introvert, on the other hand, might struggle to communicate enthusiasm adequately. I get that, and I in no way want what I have to say to be construed as meaning you must act in a way that is not true to your nature and temperament. I have a profound respect for the way that God has created us as uniquely-talented communicators of the gospel.

However, passion in your preaching is incredibly important for several reasons:

1. Passion is compelling.

If I asked you to talk about your favorite team's big win, your latest super-awesome vacation you just returned from, the best book you ever read or movie you ever seen, chances are you would describe it in a way that was effusive with energy. Even the most reserved person in the world, if you get them talking on the right subject, can talk excitedly for quite a while. When we are eager or passionate about something, it makes what we are saying compelling or more difficult to ignore.

Wow, maybe I need to read that book also!

Wow, I should rent that movie!

Wow, maybe your team is the greatest that has ever stepped foot on the diamond, the court, or the gridiron.

When we preach, our passion makes what we are saying more compelling. I love the old statement that a preacher should preach as a dying man to dying men. There's a lot of wisdom in that. If our audience discerns that some things in life excite us more than the gospel of Jesus Christ, it will deeply inhibit our ability to sway them in spiritual matters. But when they see God and his Word genuinely ignite within us an unparalleled fire of enthusiasm, it makes our message all the more compelling.

2. Passion is contagious.

I like being around passionate people because I know they will rub off on me. I have a friend who preaches in Tennessee, and I love every moment I get to spend with him because his enthusiasm about everything is contagious. He has the ability to talk me into almost anything because he's always ridiculously, but genuinely, excited about it. And am I ever thankful that his passion is expended on the things of God!

Passion is contagious. If our preaching is passionate and enthusiastic, it can't help but stir the hearts of our audience. If, however, we preach about the bread of life, yet it looks like it has given us indigestion and we need a bottle of Pepto, then our congregation will not benefit very much from our preaching. I've sat through sermons that had no passion, no spirit, no drive, and I left seriously thinking about converting to Buddhism.

Not really, but you get my point.

3. Passion is convicting.

When I was in high school, my speech teacher showed us several videos of famous world leaders giving speeches. He wanted us to learn the principles of skilled communicators. One of the videos was of Adolf Hitler giving a political speech to the German people in the 1930s. I couldn't understand a word he said since it was in German, but whatever Hitler was saying, he was fired up about it. I remember thinking, "No wonder Germany bought into his inflammatory rhetoric and diabolical plans." Hitler's passion was convicting, a successful call to action. Sadly, that call to action led a nation to hell and the world into war.

Passion in our preaching will inevitably convict the hearts of our audience. I've heard sermons by men whose passion for Christ was evident to all. So committed were they to the gospel of Christ that their enthusiasm seemed to ooze from their pores, and I found myself yearning for some reason or other to respond to the invitation! On the other hand, we've all heard (and preached) sermons after which not even the tenderest hearts felt the need to respond.

When I reflect on passion in preaching, my mind inevitably goes to Paul. There may not be a greater defense of his preaching ministry than in 2 Corinthians. In 5:6-8, he speaks of being of "good courage" in his ministry. To me, that translates into "passion."

In the opening of this chapter, I confessed that I was incapable of inspiring passion in anyone long-term, let alone myself. But there are some biblical truths that, when considered, fan the flames of my heart and inject a lot more passion in my preaching. The passion that these truths bring is a genuine, long-lasting passion because they are rooted in Christ. Beginning in 2 Cor. 5:10, the apostle hits on a few of these truths.

Our passion is inspired by...

jesus' wrath

> For we must all appear before the judgment seat of Christ, so that each one may receive what is due for what he has done in the body, whether good or evil. Therefore, knowing the fear of the Lord, we persuade others.
>
> 2 Cor. 5:10-11

In the opening chapter of his book *The Jesus I Never Knew*, Philip Yancey talks about how many people's conception of Jesus is just a stone's throw away from Mister Rogers or Captain Kangaroo. In the gospels, Yancey says, Jesus comes across to some as a Charles Dickens' character, going around patting children on the head.

I certainly think that the image of Christ in the gospels is somewhat different from the way he is depicted in his post-resurrection, now-ascended, glorified state at the Father's right hand. In Revelation, for example, Jesus appeared to John, and the apostle became like a dead man (1:17). Later in the book, he fearsomely appears on a white war horse with sword in hand, fire in his eyes, and eager to trounce his enemies furiously as if they are grapes in God's winepress (19:11-15).

My point is that Jesus is a figure to be feared as much as he is to be loved and cherished. Throughout his writings, Paul's use of "Lord" often refers to Christ. I guess I mention that because I've always read 2 Cor. 5:11 and thought Paul was talking about the fear of *God* (i.e. the Father). But I think he has the fear or terror of *Jesus* in mind. It is Jesus' judgment seat before which everyone will one day appear, and that is a dreadful thought. When he would extend the invitation after his sermons, my dad used to remind the audience, "Jesus wants to be your Savior and Lord. One day, he will be your Judge. Don't meet him as Judge without first knowing him as Savior and Lord."

Good advice.

Today's preacher, as God's messenger or mouthpiece, takes his place in a lineage that began with the Old Testament prophets. Though it is never easy, and certainly should never be enjoyable, our commission is to warn the world of the coming "Day of the Lord," a theme in the prophets that points to the decisive day when God will pour out judgment on the wicked. The word Paul uses in 2 Cor. 5:11 that is translated "fear" in the ESV is the Greek *phobos*, from which we get our English word "phobia." The apostle has in mind a fear-filled shrinking back from Christ because we are too guilty, and he is too holy. Knowing what it's like to shrink back from Jesus, Paul says he persuades men to make things right before it's eternally too late.

This past summer, the ALS ice bucket challenge became a social-media sensation. A few years ago, a former New Orleans Saints football player named Steve Gleason was diagnosed with ALS. No one knows how much time Gleason has to live on this earth, but it probably won't be very long. Because of that, Steve Gleason has made it his life's mission to warn people about the effects of ALS, and to help raise both awareness of and funds for discovering a cure for ALS. If Gleason had campaigned for ALS before his diagnosis, he probably would have done some good, but his work wouldn't have been as memorable, nor would he be as passionate. But he knows the terrible effects of ALS because he lives with it daily and will likely die from it, barring the discovery of a cure.

Our passion in preaching partly derives from our personal consideration of the wrath and terror of Jesus. As students of the Word, we should reflect mournfully and fearfully over passages such as 2 Cor. 5:10-11, 2 Thess. 1:6-9, and Rev. 19:11-15 that warn of Jesus' wrath. We must not allow our audience to develop a one-sided (and thereby stunted) view of Jesus. They must also be made to anticipate Christ's fearful wrath if they meet him as Judge without his already being their Savior and Lord.

jesus' love

> For the love of Christ controls us, because we have concluded this: that one has died for all, therefore all have died;
>
> 2 Cor. 5:14

The only other occasion in the New Testament where the word "control" (Greek *sunecho*) is used in this way is Acts 18:5, where we find that Paul in Corinth "was occupied [*sunecho*] with the word, testifying to the Jews that the Christ was Jesus." The word, according to Bauer, meant "to occupy someone's attention intensely ... to provide impulse for some activity ... to hold within bounds so as to manage or guide."

As we reflect on Jesus' wrath that is being stored up for the final day, we realize that all of us, even preachers (and maybe especially preachers!) deserve the worst of God's fury that will be poured out on sinners. Paul once referred to himself as the chief of sinners (1 Tim. 1:15), and I admit there are days when I embarrassingly think I might be next in line. But God's grace to me as poured out through the person and work of Christ is nothing short of amazing, and Christ's love indeed compels or controls me. All around me, I see evidence of how much Jesus loves me, of how faithful he has been to me and my family.

One of the dangerous ruts a preacher can fall into is when he only reads Scripture to prepare for a class or sermon or devotional. Seldom is the occasion (unless we make time for it intentionally) when we read Scripture for our own edification. As I think about Paul in Corinth with his attention intensely occupied by the Word of Christ, I realize my passion for the gospel will depend upon my personal experience with it. I cannot be passionate in my preaching when the Word's impact on my life has only been for the purpose of preaching. If the only reason I read the Bible is because it's my job, I'll have a job-like mentality in the pulpit, and everyone in the audience will quickly catch on. But if, like Paul, the gospel and love of Christ consume my attention and compel or urge or inspire me toward action in every arena of life, then this will bleed through when I proclaim the sacred message each Lord's day.

jesus' work

> Therefore, if anyone is in Christ, he is a new creation. The old has passed away; behold, the new has come.
>
> 2 Cor. 5:17

Another of the worst ruts a preacher can fall into in his preaching is when he becomes a dispenser of spiritual trivia, rather than an agent or instrument of God's transforming power in the hearts of the lost. Admit it: there have been times when you were more excited to share some great insight you had discerned in study than the prospect that a life might be changed by the message preached. I know I've been guilty of that. I spent hours during the week trying to come up with something mind-blowing, seeking to impress people and merit their applause. I forgot, however, that the goal of preaching is to transform hearts by God power, not impress minds with my stellar acumen.

New Years is always an exciting time for me, and for more reasons than there is a lot of college football bowl games to watch. I like the opportunity to start fresh, to turn over a new leaf, to resolve to kick some bad habits and institute new ones. People like New Years since it offers a new start, a clean slate, a fresh calendar. But many of us quickly abandon our New Year's resolutions before the calendar turns to February. The glory of preaching is that we are able to offer a people a fresh start on life, one that comes through the transforming power of God. When someone is in Christ, they are equipped and empowered to put off the old and take on the new by the same might that raised Jesus from the dead (cf. Rom. 8:11). This isn't a magic that comes from eating black-eyed peas or trying really hard.

It is a divine power from God.

As a preacher, it is difficult not to become cynical about the possibilities of change. We stand and speak, Sunday after Sunday, but seldom notice any real change or response to the gospel's call. When I preach a sermon on a given subject— some sin or problem I perceive in the church—I expect that issue to be neutralized after preaching on it once. Am I the only one who is frustrated when that doesn't happen!?

God's work in the hearts of our audience is no different than his work in us—it's slow; glacially slow at times. You can't microwave spiritual discipleship. The God who waited until Abraham was 75 and Moses was 80 is rarely in a hurry with anyone today. And if I'm honest, it takes a while for *me* to get on board with how God wants me to change. It can take months or even years! The faithful presentation of God's Word to my heart is what makes the difference. God wears me down, and I finally submit to the painful, but necessary, process of spiritual renovation.

God's work in our audience is no different. Our passion in preaching derives somewhat from the knowledge that God is shaping our audience into new creatures, but that's a slow process. We play our part by faithfully presenting the Word, week in and week out, until God's work is completed in the hearts of his people (Phil. 1:6). I'm just grateful and passionate about being part of that process!

jesus' commission

> Therefore, we are ambassadors for Christ, God making his appeal through us. We implore you on behalf of Christ, be reconciled to God.
>
> 2 Cor. 5:20

The act of preaching is a holy endeavor because, when

God decided to redeem and reconcile himself with the world, he chose to make known his plan through the act of preaching. As I've often heard it said, God had one son and he made him a preacher (Mark 1:38). In 2 Cor. 5:20, Paul uses a word of honor and distinction, one of respectability, when he says that he and his co-workers in ministry are "ambassadors for Christ." Our passion in preaching should derive from the reality that God has commissioned us as his ambassadors to make his will known to the world. And we have been tasked with a very glorious message, that God no longer wishes to be enemies with his people, but to be reconciled.

God does not get angry over sin the way you and I get angry. When I get angry, it's often for a bad reason. My anger is habitually irrational. If I hurt or damage anything in my anger, it's only so that I will feel better about things. But God's anger over sin is a completely different matter altogether. His anger over sin is just. And when we sinned against him the first time, he became angry. Like Adam and Eve, we were forced from his presence. If that separation lasted for all eternity, it would only be our fault. But God didn't want it to be that way forever, so he sent Christ to redeem us and reconcile us to himself. God poured out on Jesus all his wrath that should have been poured out on us. While on the cross, Jesus experienced the full force of God's punishment deserved by murderers, liars, adulterers, homosexuals, alcoholics, thieves, embezzlers, dictators, you, and me. And because "he made him to be sin who knew no sin," you and I have the hope of being reconciled to God.

Brother, you and I get to preach that message of merciful grace and faithful love each week. How can our passion not be inflamed by such a great hope!?

At the end of the day, Christ and his good-news message are what ignite and fuel our passion in preaching. If you've been injecting passion into your preaching through short-lived means, give up now and root your passion in Christ! If anything else excites you about preaching—the adulation, fame, recognition, prestige that sometimes comes to preachers—then your passion will one day fail you. If you are preaching for yourself, you likely won't be preaching very long.

But if it is Christ that pulls and pushes you forward—if it is Christ that compels and controls you—then you'll never have to fake your enthusiasm or passion. It will be apparent to all who hear you speak about the mysteries of Christ.

And your Father in heaven will be glorified.

6

better balance
jay lockhart

An elderly woman who had been a member of the Lord's church for decades said, "Preachers are not preaching the Bible like they once did, and they are not being trained as they once were." She was right, you know! Some schools that are said to specialize in the training of preachers are emphasizing manner over message, style over substance, and pragmatism over preaching. Perhaps at no time in the history of the church in America has there been a greater need for balance in ministry than right now.

what is balance?

For the purpose of this chapter "balance" will be defined as "equality of emphasis placed upon various parts of the whole" (see Webster, 105-106). The last book Ira North wrote emphasized balance in our service to God. In illustrating balance, North referred to the statement found in Hosea 7:8

which says, "Ephraim is a cake not turned." He went on to say that in Old Testament times, a cake was made by pouring the batter on heated rocks, and if the cake was not turned at the proper time, it would be doughy on one side and burned on the other (North, 10). In a similar way, if an individual, a congregation, or a preacher is not balanced in the work which needs to be done, the outcome will be that some good things will be neglected, while other good things will be over emphasized. A good question for all of us to ask as we are involved in the work of the church is, "Am I giving 'equality of emphasis' to all that needs to be done? " Of course, some things are more important than others, but in keeping with the relative importance of what needs to be done, we must be balanced.

balance in the preacher's life

It will be difficult for the preacher to be balanced in his preaching until he is balanced in other areas of his life. First, the preacher must find a balance between continuing education and his work in ministry. Some preachers may not have a desire to receive formal education beyond their initial training in the classroom. However, if he does pursue continuing education the preacher must find balance. He must not neglect the people in his congregation because he is pursuing additional formal training. Some important aspects of working with a congregation is to know the people, to share in the joys and sorrows of the people, and to minister to the people. The preacher will be much more effective in the pulpit if he has a genuine interest in the lives of the people on other days in the week. This also applies to the preacher's family. He must strike a balance between his work and the need to allot an appropriate amount of time to being a husband and father. The Shulamite said in the Song of Solomon, "They made me keeper of the vineyards, but my own vineyard I have not kept!" (Song 1:6). In seeking to save the world, the preacher must not neglect the salvation of his own family. Additionally, the preacher must find a balance between recreation and work. Every preacher needs some time during the week to lay aside his usual duties and to relax by doing something not related to his work of ministry. However, he should remember that three days a week on the golf course or at his favorite fishing hole is somewhat excessive.

balance in the preacher's work

Effective preaching is hard work, and if the preacher desires to work with one church for an extended period of time, he must be diligent in his studies, in his excitement for preaching, and in his freshness in presenting his lessons. To do this, the preacher must allocate large blocks of time to sermon and Bible class preparation and delivery. After all, the preacher's work is preaching. He is not called to visitation (although that is an important part of ministry). He is not called to be a counselor (although he will be thrust into situations where he will help people work through difficulties, where he will help them prepare for marriage, and where he will give advice in many areas of their lives). He is not called to be a comedian or an after-dinner speaker (although there is a time and a place for laughter and non-biblical speech making). In addition to preaching, there are numerous other things a preacher is to do. These things include someone who needs a personal Bible study, or someone in the congregation who has unexpected surgery, or who has an accident, or who has died. And then there is the person from the congregation who has an hour to waste and chooses to waste it with the preacher. These things are a part of the preacher's life, and adjustments must be made. However, he must compensate for these things by finding adequate time for study by getting up earlier in the morning, or by turning off the computer or television, or by staying up later at night. The preacher's work is preaching, and he must find adequate time for preparation.

balance in the preacher's preaching

Seeing the Big Picture

As one prepares for balance in preaching, there are a number of issues that must be considered.

1. Preaching must be defined. What is preaching? John A. Broadus, who wrote and spoke so much about preaching, defined preaching as "proclamation through personality." While this is not a full definition, it does emphasize the fact that preaching has to do with the message and the messenger. The power of preaching is in the message, but the message cannot be separated from the "earthen vessels" (2 Cor. 4:7) who speak the message. However, the vessels must never get in the way of the message. Two New Testament words that define preaching are *euaggelidzo*, meaning "to bring good news, to announce glad tidings" (Thayer, 256), and *kerusso*, meaning "to proclaim to persons one with whom they are to become acquainted in order to learn what they are to do" (Thayer, 346). Preaching must proclaim the good news of what God has accomplished for lost humanity through Jesus Christ. It is true that, in preaching, there is a time to "convince" and "rebuke" (2 Tim. 4:2), but first and foremost, preaching is to announce good news. Additionally, preaching must proclaim Christ (the one with whom we are to become acquainted) and must show hearers how to obey Christ (learn what they are to do). Therefore, preaching is to encounter God Himself (see Lockhart, *The Preacher*, 169).

2. *The message of preaching must be understood.* To Timothy, Paul said, "Preach the word" (2 Tim. 4:2). To the elders of the church at Ephesus, Paul recounted he had not shunned "from declaring to you the whole counsel of God" (Acts 20:27). To preach "the word" (*logos*) means to proclaim "the doctrine concerning the attainment through Christ of salvation in the Kingdom of God" (Thayer, 381). The word "counsel" (*boule*) is defined as "the purpose of God respecting the salvation of men through Christ. ... All the content of the Divine plan" (Thayer, 104-105). To the Romans, Paul affirmed he had fully preached the gospel of Christ (15:19). The term "fully" (*pleroo*) has a variety of meanings, such as, "to fill, make full, fulfill, complete or finish" (O'Brien, 82). In the Romans passage, Paul may have had in mind the finishing of his commission received from the Lord to fully take the gospel to the Gentiles. But the same root is used in Col. 1:25 to refer to the message preached so that the Gentiles might believe and obey the gospel in order that they could be presented to God perfect in Christ (see Col. 1:24-29). For this to be done, the full or complete message was preached by Paul and must be preached by us (Gal. 1:6-9). There is no teaching of Scripture that the preacher will not preach or that he neglects to preach.

The implications here are far-reaching because the preacher who fails to biblically answer the question, "What must I do to be saved?" or who never preaches on how to worship God, the nature and identity of the New Testament church, the role of women in the church, why we sing without mechanical accompaniment in worship, and a myriad of other basic and fundamental Bible subjects is failing to preach the gospel.

Further, Paul said to the Corinthians, "I decided to know nothing among you except Jesus Christ and him crucified" (1 Cor. 2:2). When Paul said he knew nothing but Christ crucified, he was using a synecdoche, "a figure of speech in which a part is used for the whole" (Webster, 1444). Examples of this are found in other places in the New Testament as when the first-century church was "breaking bread in their homes" (Acts 2:46; clearly a reference to having a meal together which included more than just bread; see also Acts 20:11). Also, the Lord's Supper is referred to as "to break bread" (Acts 20:7), even though the Supper included the fruit of the vine as well. The context must determine if the breaking of bread refers to the Lord's Supper or to a common meal.

Notice how inclusive the preaching of Christ and Him crucified is.

1. Preaching Christ crucified places the emphasis of preaching upon the message more than upon the messenger, which is what Paul did (see 1 Cor. 2:1, 3-5).

2. Preaching Christ crucified focuses man's predicament of sin since "Christ died for our sins" (1 Cor. 15:3).

3. Preaching Christ crucified emphasizes the marvelous plan of God in saving us from our sins (1 Cor. 1:18).

4. Preaching Christ crucified shows the efficacy of the blood of Christ in cleansing us from our sins (Matt. 26:28; Eph. 1:7).

5. Preaching Christ crucified is to proclaim the "wisdom of God" which is the whole purpose

and plan of God to save men and has been made known to us by the revelation and inspiration of the Holy Spirit (1 Cor. 2:7-13).

Indeed, to preach Christ crucified includes "the whole spectrum of the inspired revelation of God, including salvation, the church, and Christian living" (Lockhart, "Christ and Him Crucified," 3-5). The message is the entire word of God.

3. *The preacher's view of Scripture must be analyzed.* The preacher must believe the message of the Bible is all the truth pertaining to God's will for man (John 17:17; 16:13). Further, he must accept Scripture as the final (Jude 3), complete (2 Tim. 3:16-17), authoritative (1 Pet. 4:11), and inspired word of the living God (1 Cor. 2:7-13). If he does not believe these things, he has no message, and balance becomes a mute point.

4. *What most people in the pews are looking for must be considered.* The cry of some that "if we are to interest people in today's culture, we must give them what they want" is not my experience. We believe that most people attending our assemblies are asking, "Is there any word from the LORD? " (Jer. 37:17). The people coming to our assemblies have faced the world all week, and they do not come to worship looking for a circus, or to hear a comedian, or to be brought up to date on current events. They come to hear a "word from the Lord. " And the word that they hear from the Lord must be a balanced diet which will help them grow in their spiritual lives.

5. *Meeting the real needs of people must be a priority.* The mindset of the culture is that the "felt needs" of people must be met. However, preaching should meet the "real needs" which people have. And what are these "real needs"? First and foremost, every person needs to be saved from sin. And God's plan to meet this need is the gospel. Paul said to the Romans

that the gospel is "the power of God for salvation" (Rom. 1:16). The Book of Romans develops

- what the gospel is (1:1-17)
- the universal need of the gospel (1:18-3:20)
- the explanation of the gospel (3:21-31)
- the illustration of biblical faith which is produced by the gospel (4:1-25)
- the provision of salvation (5:1-21)
- how salvation is accepted (6:1-23)
- freedom in Christ (7:1-25)
- how the gospel is lived out in our lives (8:1-39; 12:1ff).

The pure gospel of Christ must be preached in order that people may know how their greatest need can be satisfied.

Second, when the greatest need is met, the next greatest need of people must be satisfied. That need is to grow and develop as a Christian. This growth is made possible through the study and application of Scripture. Paul put it this way: "I commend you to God and to the word of his grace, which is able to build you up and to give you the inheritance among all those who are sanctified." (Acts 20:32). Preaching God's word can meet this second greatest need of humanity. When the issues mentioned above have been considered and settled, the preacher is prepared to address balance in his preaching.

Balance in Preaching

1. The preacher should examine his preaching over the last five years. If he has been in his present position for less than five years, let him consider what he has preached since beginning his present work. Next, categorize the sermons according to the subject matter. If the preacher finds that he is preaching for a well-established congregation, and that he preached a dozen sermons which were mostly about how to become Christian and only two sermons on Christian maturity, he may need to be more balanced. If he finds he has preached a dozen times on man's responsibility in saving himself, but only two times on what God has done for us, he may need to see if he is balanced in his preaching. This is just something we need to consider because circumstances do alter the subject in biblical preaching.

2. The preacher should plan what themes need to be developed in the coming year. He may discover that he needs to preach a series of messages on worship, a series on the family, a series on leadership, or that he needs to preach through a biblical book. Series preaching is always subject to interruption if some special need arises through the year, but this kind of planning can be most helpful. It allows the preacher to know where he is going in his preaching, and he can gather materials through his reading and study that will help him in developing the individual sermons in the series. Preaching through a biblical book helps the preacher to be balanced, because he preaches on subjects that he might not tackle otherwise. After all, if a subject comes up in preaching through a book, he has to deal with it. Planning one's preaching for a year at a time, though through the year he will probably need to make adjustments, is wise and helpful in many ways. For example, if a preacher knows he is going to present a certain series of sermons in the last quarter of the year, he can be gathering materials for that series from now until it is time to present the sermons. If the preacher will be balanced, let him examine where he has been in his preaching, and let him know where he wishes to go.

3. The preacher should make every effort to preach the

whole counsel of God. This should include preaching from the Old Testament as well as the New Testament. "For whatever was written in former days was written for our instruction" (Rom. 15:4). Preach those things! Preach the great themes of the Bible. This includes such things as the majesty of God, the identity of Jesus, the words of the Holy Spirit, the nature and identity of the New Testament church, the meaning of discipleship, how to worship God, the what, who, and why of baptism, leadership roles in the church, how one is saved, the restoration of New Testament Christianity, and on and on. There must be no theme upon which the preacher will not preach, and he must constantly be examining his preaching to make sure he is preaching on a broad range of subjects.

4. The preacher must balance the positive and the negative. There are times to rebuke, and there are times to exhort, but always with patience (2 Tim. 4:2). The enemy is not in the pew. The people to whom we speak are often struggling, hurting, and needing help. When the preacher seeks to enter their situation and to present help for their lives from God's word, he should be more positive and upbeat than negative and harsh. People are people, and there will always be those who do not behave properly, but to bash those who are present because of the behavior of those who may not be present may do more harm than good. It should be remembered that in every congregation, there are good people who are trying to live right, and the preacher should be helping them develop into the image of Christ. There are things right with each local congregation, and these things need to be discovered and encouraged. When the preacher feels compelled to deal with a problem he sees in the congregation, he should do it with compassion and the skill of the surgeon rather than with anger and hatefulness.

In dealing with the church at Thessalonica Paul said, "But

we were gentle among you, like a nursing mother taking care of her own children. ... For you know how, like a father with his children, we exhorted each one of you and encouraged you and charged you to walk in a manner worthy of God, who calls you into his own kingdom and glory" (1 Thess. 2:7, 11-12). If the preacher's message is mostly negative, the people will likely fail to hear and will not be drawn closer to the Lord. It should be remembered that if one rejects the word of the Lord, he will answer to God for it, but if one turns away from the Lord because of the caustic attitude of the preacher, it becomes the responsibility of the preacher. Let us keep in mind that whatever the problem may be with which we are dealing, we must speak "the truth in love" (Eph. 4:15). I am convinced that if people know that the preacher loves them, he can say anything that needs to be said and the people will hear him. Balance the positive with the negative and seek to be more positive and encouraging than negative and harsh.

5. *Balance in preaching can be achieved when the preacher keeps in mind that there is power in the gospel to change people* (Rom. 1:16; 1 Cor. 1:18). Paul put it this way: "For what we proclaim is not ourselves, but Jesus Christ as Lord, with ourselves as your servants for Jesus' sake. ... But we have this treasure in jars of clay, to show that the surpassing power belongs to God and not to us" (2 Cor. 4:5, 7). If those who preach will remember that the power to transform people, including themselves, is in the message more than in the messenger, then they will seek to preach "the whole counsel of God" with balance as they allow the word of the Lord, preached in its fullness, to change the world.

works cited

Lockhart, Jay. "Christ and Him Crucified." *The Spiritual Sword* 40/2 (Jan. 2009).

—. "What I Have Learned In Over Fifty Years Of Preaching." *The Preacher and His Work*. Ed. Dr. David Powell, 2013.

North, Ira. *Balance*. Nashville: Gospel Advocate, 1983.

O'Brian, Peter T. *Word Biblical Commentary*, Vol. 44, "Colossians, Philemon." Waco, TX: Word Books, 1982.

Thayer, Henry. *A Greek-English Lexicon of the New Testament*. Chicago: American Book Company, n.d.

Webster's New World Dictionary. New York: Simon and Schuster, 1986.

7

better application
jacob hawk

With fire in his bones, the preacher climbs into the saddle of the pulpit. His knees shake. His palms are sweaty. His voice crackles like wood in a fire. The next 25-30 minutes (because face it—that's the longest people will listen to you, regardless of how "dynamic" you are) will either be a walk-off homerun or a sit-down strikeout.

Is he adequately prepared? Yes.

Is his heart in the right place? Sure.

Has he prayed that God will use the message for His glory? Always.

There's just one thing that isn't a slam dunk, and he knows it—application. That's why he's so nervous. That's the one part of the sermon we don't teach because it's so difficult to explain.

You can't teach someone to "apply" like you teach them to outline. You can't teach someone to convict hearts like you teach them to exegete the text. You can't teach someone to unpack relevance like you teach them to translate Greek.

Also, application varies from place to place. What applies

to a church in Texas may not apply to a church in New York. What applies to a retired majority may not apply to a working minority. Application must be modified or adapted from one context to another.

That's why our universities and preaching schools don't teach application in depth—they can't. It's not their fault, nor is it laziness on their part. They simply realize what all preachers should know—better application only comes with experience. The more you preach, the better you get. And to be completely honest, it can be a painful lesson to learn.

With that being said, please allow me to share a few "tips" I've learned throughout my preaching career. These lessons have been learned through the bruises and scrapes of the brethren. That might be a little extreme, but as I said in the previous paragraph, learning to use better application can be painful. Trust me. I've been there. I hope that my pain will result in your gain. For better application…

know your audience better

Remember the preacher I mentioned at the beginning with shaky knees, sweaty palms, and a crackling voice, even though he's years past puberty? That used to be me. People never knew it, but it was. Some Sundays, I was scared to death.

I'm not that way anymore. I still get butterflies in my stomach, but it's not caused by fear, just excitement. That's because I have the confidence to do what I couldn't do when I first started preaching. I can build a bridge for my listeners from the biblical world to our world today.

You can preach with great eloquence, offer incredible insights, tell the funniest jokes, and give the most startling statistics. But if you can't answer the question, "So what?" your sermon is sunk—and there's no way you're ever bringing it back to the surface.

Our churches want to know why all of this biblical "talk" matters. What can they take home with them today that will change their life tomorrow? What can they do this week to bring their co-workers to church next week? Enter our friend, application. He answers those questions every time.

But if you want better application, you have to know your people better. That doesn't mean you have to know every struggle in their lives; some things will always remain confidential. It does mean, however, that you need to know your audience and respect your arena.

My first ministry setting was a small, rural country town in Texas. I grew up in Dallas. This quickly proved to be a bad combination for a novice preacher trying to learn the ropes of application. I remember asking my audience one Sunday, "You know what it's like getting stuck in rush hour?" No, they didn't know what it was like. The heaviest rush hour they experienced was getting stuck behind some longhorns trying to cross the road from one pasture to the next. *Bad* application. They knew it. I knew it. And I was the one with the red face.

I can't be too hard on myself, though. All preachers make these mistakes. One of my favorite examples is my dad when he first started ministry. As a youth intern, the very first class he taught was to a group of 7th grade boys on a Sunday evening. What did he choose for his topic? 1 Cor. 7—marriage, divorce, and re-marriage. I'm sure those boys were itching to know why they could/could not get a divorce, and the freedoms that they would enjoy or be refused once they entered bachelorhood.

A great application is actually applicable. That sounds so elementary, but that basic truth is often overlooked. If you want to convict your hearers, know your hearers. It will make a world of difference.

know your context better

To know your context, you don't just know your people. You also know your passage.

As bad as it is to be ignorant about who you're talking to, it's even worse to be ignorant about what you're discussing. Biblical writers, inspired by the Holy Spirit, wrote what they wrote, to whom they wrote it, for a reason. Don't change that reason. Don't twist their context to fit your context. Just as you preach a passage in the way it was meant to be preached, apply the passage in the way it was meant to be applied.

An example I have used in other books, but one which I think makes the point so well, is Phil. 4:13. It's one of the most misused verses in the entire Bible. It's not because the verse is misunderstood, but misapplied. Paul says he can do all things through Christ because of his comments in the previous verses about learning to be content! When we finally learn to be content (which some people never learn), that's when we can do (or endure) all things through Christ. Consequently, some people will never be able to do all things through Christ because they won't learn to be content.

I've seen numerous posters of Michael Jordan or LeBron James dunking a basketball with Phil. 4:13 inscribed at the top. As I wrote in my book, *When Mountains Won't Move*, God doesn't care if you can dunk a basketball. God cares about holiness and righteousness. If being able to do all things through Christ gives me the ability to dunk a basketball, I must not have Christ in me. I have as good a chance of dunking a basketball as Mother Theresa.

Jesus uses powerful application in the parables. As we've always heard, these were earthly stories with heavenly meanings; even though their meaning was heavenly, they were applicable on earth. One of my favorite parables, which is easy to apply, is found in Luke 18:1-8. Jesus tells the parable of the persistent widow.

For that audience, it applied to them like a glove fits a hand. Many of Jesus' hearers were poor, just like that widow. Many of His hearers had no one to speak in their defense, just like that widow. The Jews were the doormat for the Romans' dirty boots. Therefore, the only tool in their bag of tricks was persistence.

It's the same message for the church today. The church can't, or at least shouldn't, get its way through financial prowess. The church has no one to speak in its defense except Jesus Christ. Therefore, the only tool in our spiritual reserve is persistence. We go to God time and time again, knowing that He never grows weary of hearing from His children. What a blessing!

Recently, I used this passage to preach a sermon entitled, "The Parable of the Persistent American." Much of our membership is politically oriented. They're very concerned about the direction our country is currently taking, especially when it comes to morals and spirituality. Therefore, before the 2014 mid-term elections, I preached this sermon with this framework. If we're so concerned about our country, let's be persistent Americans, praying that justice will come, and come quickly. It may not happen on our watch or our time table, but when it does happen, the Son of Man will find faith on earth (Luke 18:8) when He hears the prayers of His people. The sermon was very well received, but not because of my scholarly presentation. It was received well because it applied well.

If you want better application, know your context better. To borrow from the words of James, a fig tree doesn't bear olives and a grapevine doesn't bear figs (Jas. 3:12). An application can't enlighten a passage where it doesn't apply.

know yourself better

I don't mean that you should know your limitations, your likes and dislikes, or even your strengths and weaknesses when it comes to the delivery of your sermon. What I'm suggesting is that all preachers need to know that they're saints, but that they're also sinners—just like our listeners who sit in our pews.

The apostle Paul didn't struggle to "know" himself. In 1 Tim. 1:15, Paul said he was the worst of all sinners—the "chief" sinner according to some translations. I believe with all of my heart that our congregations yearn to hear that their preachers struggle with the same things they do. It's very dangerous when we place preachers on a pedestal. Not only is it unfair to the preacher and his family; it's unfair to the congregation. In doing so, we place our confidence in the speaker rather than the Savior.

At the same time, I realize Scripture says preachers should set an example (1 Tim. 4:12), and that's certainly fair. If you're going to preach the Word of God, you need to not only know the Word, but live it. James even tells us that, as teachers and preachers, we will be judged more strictly (Jas. 3:1).

But there's a happy medium and an honorable balance. Preachers should be men of integrity and faith, but both integrity and faith are built on humility. Humility is at its best when it's put to the test, and the test comes when we confess our struggles.

I was very blessed to grow up sitting at the feet of Robert K. Oglesby, one of the greatest preachers the church has ever known. His innovative preaching style, his longevity in location

(52 years in one place), and his love for people and for deep, spiritual growth were evident throughout his ministry. As a little boy, I even remember asking my parents on Sundays if he was God. His voice echoed with authority, but soothed with love. He was one of my biggest heroes and still is to this day.

During my first ministry job, I was able to see Robert in a different capacity. He came to our small church in Llano, Texas to host a Group Discussion Seminar, just like he had been doing for decades for churches all around the country. During that weekend, he stayed in our home. My wife and I thoroughly enjoyed the time spent in our living room with Robert and his wife, Willora. While drinking some coffee and enjoying some pie, Robert and I discussed ministry and the struggles that each of us faced. I sat and listened in awe.

At that time, this man, who had been preaching at the same congregation for 47 years, faced the same struggles I faced in my first year in Llano. Granted, the struggles might have been on a different scale or for a different reason, but they were the same struggles. In that moment, I realized I wasn't alone. My hero hurt just like me. And because of that, in my heart, he was an even bigger hero.

I witnessed a similar event happen in my own ministry. The move to Kerrville was great for our family. We went to a much bigger church with different challenges. This was no longer a small country church—it was a congregation filled with retired executives, school teachers, bankers, doctors, financial consultants, coaches, and most intimidating—retired ministers. In Llano, if you misquoted a passage and if someone noticed, they would smile. In Kerrville, they would certainly notice, and a smile wasn't their usual response.

I remember it like it was yesterday. In October 2013, I preached a sermon entitled, "Fact or Friend? " In that sermon, I argued that many Christians know the Word (Scripture), but they don't truly know *the Word* (Jesus). It's very easy to view Jesus as a fact that we quote, rather than a friend whom we cherish. As the sermon was coming to a close, I moved to the application of the sermon, where success or failure hinges on the preacher's ability to apply. With fear in my heart (and I'm sure in my voice), I confessed to my church family that for too long, I had viewed Jesus simply as a fact. I had two degrees in Bible. I had written some books. I had preached several sermons, and I had taught many classes. The fact was present, but the relationship was absent. And this unfortunate truth brought more pain into my life than I was willing to continue to bear—at least privately. I was very nervous standing in the foyer after services that morning, worrying about how my sermon was going to be accepted.

I kept thinking to myself, "Will people lose respect for me?"

"Will the elders call a special meeting to rebuke me?"

"Will people stop coming to me for advice because I've fallen from some spiritual peak?"

Not at all. Respect was gained. No elder's meeting convened. People were very supportive.

I don't tell this story to pat myself on the back, because I have no reason to pat. I'm a sinner. Even though I preach the Word, I struggle to practice what I preach. The day that preachers no longer struggle to practice what they've preached is the day they should surrender the pulpit, because their preaching has lost its power. The struggle makes growth not only possible, but plausible. When we stop setting goals high, we stop thinking about heavenly things.

Preacher, I want you to know that it's okay to admit weakness, especially since you're a preacher! Paul said "I will boast all the more gladly of my weaknesses, so that the power of Christ may rest upon me" (2 Cor. 12:9). Admitting weakness was one of the things that made Paul so strong.

God knows you. Like it or not, people know you.

Know yourself better. Your applications will follow suit.

know your purpose better

Why do you step into the pulpit to preach? Hopefully, you already know that preaching has absolutely nothing to do about you—it's all about God. If you don't believe this, then please do your congregation a favor and resign. Everything—absolutely everything—needs to be done for God's glory, not yours.

Based on the facts that you're reading a book about preaching and that you want to be a better preacher, I'm confident you realize this. You want to be a better preacher so you can serve God better, and you should be commended for that.

Since the most important purpose has been clarified, let me ask again, why do you step into the pulpit to preach?

- To educate? That's certainly important. Our congregations need a good, solid education about biblical doctrines so they can know what a Christian is and isn't.
- To inform? That's equally important. People need to not only learn, but they need to be reminded.
- To rebuke? Be careful on this one, preacher. There's a mile-long list about the right way to rebuke, and don't ever convince yourself that it's your job to police or judge. That job belongs to God—you don't have the credentials. Yes, a loving rebuke is sometimes necessary, but that can't be your main purpose.

There's one goal that you must accomplish in the sermon, which unfortunately often gets neglected: motivate. Do you remember what I said at the beginning of this chapter? You can preach with great eloquence, offer incredible insights, tell the funniest jokes, and give the most startling statistics; but if you can't answer the question "So what?" your sermon is sunk—and there's no way you're ever bringing it back to the surface. I believe this with every ounce of my being. I trust that you do too.

We've all listened to preachers who told us what we already knew, but left us wondering why they told us. If you just educate, inform, or rebuke, you aren't preaching—you're lecturing, and our congregations know the difference.

After Jesus washed feet in the Upper Room, and after He proved what true service is all about, He looked at His twelve apostles with pedicures and said, "If you know these things, blessed are you if you do them" (John 13:17). What's that called? Application.

If people can't hear what the last 25-30 minutes have to do with them, your sermon doesn't need to be preached. Your listeners are called to go into the world and make a difference. You rob them of their calling if you don't motivate them to do it. Application is the mortar that holds effectiveness together.

So, if you were going to develop applications that truly motivate, how would you do it? I'm certainly not an expert, but here are three things that I've found to be helpful for developing solid, motivating applications:

1. Describe the application in a way that's easy to remember.

You can do this through word pictures. You might even do it through power point or other technology mediums. Some preachers love to use alliteration or acronyms. These can also be helpful, but I would offer one word of caution about using these literary devices—don't use them too much. They can be very addictive. At one time, they were addictive for me. I found myself always wanting to force the message on my heart into some stagnant form. Use alliteration or acronyms sparingly. Then they will be surprising and effective. But after constant use, they're like your favorite ice cream that begins to taste the same. Save them for special occasions.

2. Package the application in a way that's easy to implement.

Tangible steps—a key factor to motivating applications. If you want your congregation to walk out of the doors and enter the mission field with passion, provide steps showing them how. You've been thinking about it all week. They've just heard about it for the first time. Be a true leader and draw the line for them to follow; but again, do it tangibly.

For example, if you want people to be more evangelistic, don't tell them to go down their street knocking doors. First of all, they probably don't have the courage to do it, or they would have already been doing it, negating the need for a sermon on evangelism. Secondly, in today's culture, knocking on a door is often flooded with more cons than pros.

So how do you motivate them? Remind them to start small. Maybe it's the co-worker in the office. Maybe it's the client over the phone. Maybe it's the spouse at the dinner table. It all begins with a spiritual conversation. Two minds discussing God's nature will transform into two hearts doing His will. That's a tangible step.

It works the same way with marriage, friendships, giving, and commitment. Provide tangible ways to make a difference. Allow your congregation to see that an RBI is just as good as a homerun. That will motivate them.

3. Build the application on biblical truth.

I know that's incredibly obvious, but let me explain. As we've already discussed, the purpose of an application is to motivate. There is a biblical truth which motivates everything we are and everything we want to become—we're in this together, but we'll be judged on our own.

In tip #3, we said that it's okay to know yourself by confessing fault. It's also okay for our members to do the same. They need to be reminded that as a team, we're doing our best to become living sacrifices, holy and pleasing to God (Rom. 12:1-2). However, we can't allow teamwork to erase personal responsibility. While we work together on earth, we still have to work out our own salvation (Phil. 2:12), and we will be judged based on our own lives (2 Cor. 5:10).

In years past, instilling fear was a key ingredient to successful preaching. I don't believe that scaring people is the honest way to lead them into obedience and commitment, but I do believe that reminding them of their destiny of judgment is an honorable way to apply biblical teaching. Judgment Day is coming. Preparation begins now. Make sure that sinks into their minds and heart through the sand of application. It will motivate them, and if it doesn't, the problem isn't you.

You see, application doesn't remove the fire in the bones of the preacher—it only fans the flame. The knees stop shaking. The hands stop sweating. The voice stops crackling. Application not only gives confidence; it produces conviction.

You can preach with great eloquence, offer incredible insights, tell the funniest jokes, and give the most startling statistics; but if you can't answer the question "So what?" your sermon is sunk, and there's no way you're ever bringing it back up to the surface.

Don't let your sermon sink. Application will keep you afloat.

8

better preparation
wayne roberts

"It takes a lifetime!" was my response to the question, "How long does it take you to prepare a sermon?" asked by a young preaching student. Because any given sermon is the culminating work of all that the preacher has experienced, studied, learned, and prepared. Great sermons don't just happen; they take years of preparation. Preparation is an essential part of preaching. Better preparation makes better preachers and more effective sermons.

In a professional kitchen, the chef begins his preparation with what the French call *mise en place*, which means, "Everything set in its place." Ingredients are collected, vegetables are cut, and cookware and other components are organized before any cooking takes place. In the same way, a preacher begins his sermon by collecting resources, studying passages and arranging thoughts before the sermon can be preached. This is the vital work of quality preparation. However, *mise en place* is more than just the parts of preparation, it is a mindset of the chef that understands the end objective and the arrangement of all those ingredients to gain the desired result. For both novice and seasoned preachers, the quality of the sermon will always be a reflection of the preparation put into it (or the absence of preparation). The preacher must understand the importance of preparation towards the ultimate objective of changing lives with God's word. Every step of preparation is towards this end. Better preparation takes work, and it takes time.

get on your knees

Before a page of Scripture is turned, before pen has touched paper, before a word is spoken, preparation for the sermon begins for the preacher on his knees. It would be the pinnacle of foolishness to believe that the preacher alone, even with the best oration in history, could accomplish what needs to be accomplished. God—who revealed truth, who calls men and women to come to Him, who charges men to convey His message—is the greatest assurance of success in preaching. If a good Bible student is marked by worn out Bibles, then a good preacher is marked by pants with worn out knees. The preacher will better his preparation by spending time in prayer for strength, understanding, and for those who will hear the sermon he preaches.

consider the evidence

When a CSI (Crime scene investigator) is called to a crime scene, they begin to meticulously collect and examine the evidence from the scene. The evidence is the one thing that cannot lie. It points to the truth about the case. In their study of the evidence, the CSI must be thorough and can have no personal agenda, no bias or preconceived ideas. Their only objective is to find the truth as derived from the evidence. Sermon preparation equally begins by considering the evidence. The preacher also carefully studies the "evidence," the evidence of Scripture, to determine its everlasting truths. He seeks,through his study to find the truth that God has preserved. He studies without bias or personal agenda. He seeks only to discover the truth contained within its verses. Better sermon preparation demands that the preacher identify a single truth found in a passage of Scripture, which will serve as the basis for his sermon. He studies to find the original meaning of the writer and what God is telling us throughout that writing. Scripture may have multiple applications, but it only has *one* meaning. The original writer determines the meaning; the quality Bible student discovers that meaning.

As the preacher sits in front of a blank sheet of paper or a blank computer screen with a particular sermon to be created, he asks himself, "What will I preach?", "How will I preach it?", "Where do I start?", and "What do I need to do next or first?" This is where better preparation begins. It begins with questions. There are questions about the text of Scripture, questions about the listener's needs and understanding, and questions about how to connect those two worlds through the sermon preached. No question can be left unaddressed. Whenever we view a document, whether it is a letter from our grandmother or the ingredients in our favorite breakfast cereal, we interpret the information contained in the text to determine the meaning. Much of this process goes unnoticed as we have been trained in school in language, vocabulary, context, etc. That process is made of questions that we ask ourselves as we read. Although we may not always "consciously" notice these questions, they are there nonetheless. Bible study is no different. When the preacher approaches the text, he does so seeking to determine the original meaning the author intended to convey. To understand Scripture, there are questions that he must ask. Some of these questions he may ask without really thinking about them. However, he may need to be trained to ask other questions as well. These should become part of his regular thinking when he studies the Bible. This investigative process, hermeneutics, involves a series of questions that are asked before, during, and after the study is complete. Among the investigative questions to be asked are:

- What is the historical context of the passage?
- What is the literary context of the passage?
- What is the type of literature?
- Is there figurative language being employed?
- What did the writer say?
- What did the writer mean?
- Are there direct commands of "to do's" or "not to do's"?
- Are there approved examples of how direct commands were obeyed?

Once these and questions like them are answered through study, an interpretive conclusion is made. Now the preacher can answer, "What is the truth of the passage and how does it apply to the listener?" Interpretation is not our opinion. Interpretation is the result of diligent and careful study to discover what God is saying!

Like the CSI, the preacher will and must spend more time in studying to find the truth than they will ever spend in presenting their facts.

build a bridge

Many have called the great painter, Leonardo da Vinci, "a man of two worlds" because he spanned the worlds of art and science. He was a musician, an engineer, an architect, and an artist. Preaching is both art and science. The preacher is a man of two worlds as well. He is a man who resides in both the world of Scripture and the world around him. Although he is "in the world, but not of the world," he must be a student of both worlds to effectively preach. Through the sermon, the preacher will connect the world of Scripture (truth) with the world of individual lives (application). The sermon becomes a bridge between those two worlds. Through his preaching he will build a bridge between an ancient world and a modern world, a bridge between an unknown language (Hebrew/Greek) and a familiar one, a bridge between a spiritual world and a physical one, and a bridge between God and man through the person of Jesus Christ. Once the bridge is built, and only when it is built, can an invitation be made for the listener to cross over. A bridge must be firmly anchored on each side of the span to be crossed. A sermon that focuses on Scripture alone, with a disregard for the application of those divine truths, is useless. It's like a bridge only connected on one side. A sermon that focuses on the world's needs and "relevance," with disregard to the truth of Scripture, is nothing more than a ramp that leads people to nowhere.

identify the mission

On July 20, 1969, Neil Armstrong became the first man to set foot on the moon. Years of planning and preparation had gone into the mission of that "one small step." Although there were multiple experiments performed, samples collected and other accomplishments along the way, the primary mission of Apollo 11 was to successfully land a man on the moon and return him to earth safely. Anything shy of that objective would have made the mission a failure.

Once the truth of Scripture is discovered, better sermon preparation considers the end destination or the "sermon mission" before it can continue. Until the preacher knows exactly what the purpose of the sermon is that he is preparing, he can go no further in preparation. He must ask himself, "Why am I preaching this sermon, from this text, on this occasion, to this group of listeners, and what is the action they will be asked to take?" Is the sermon going to be evangelistic, encouraging, admonishing, etc.? Is it intended to inform, to persuade, or to motivate? If he does not know where he is going in the sermon, he won't know how to get there, and no one else will either.

The mission of the sermon must also consider the listener. It considers: the mind of the listener (What knowledge and understanding will be communicated?), the heart of the listener (What belief and conviction will be developed?), and the life of the listener (What challenge will be given the listener towards obedience and godliness?). The mission considers the real-life needs of the listener and how those needs are met through Jesus. It considers how the sermon will help to shape, with the help of God's word, the listener to be more Christ-like and thus pleasing to God. It considers how the sermon will equip the listener to live a life of service to God and others. When it comes to better preparation, knowing the listener is as important as is knowing the truth of Scripture.

Every sermon must have a single mission in mind. The preacher must honestly and fully answer the question, "Why am I preaching this sermon?"

design a strategy

Whether you are climbing a mountain, crossing the country, or traveling to the moon, there must be a plan to arrive at the particular destination. That plan becomes a "map" for the trip. "Where are we now?", "Where are we going?", "What stops will we make along the way?", and "How will we get there?" A trip without a map is in danger of aimless wandering or even of missing the intended destination altogether. Every sermon needs a map as well. It needs a step-by-step process that is to be offered over the course of the sermon. It is a strategy intended to take people from where they are today to where God wants them to be over the course of the sermon (or over the course of their life). Without a deliberate strategy, the sermon risks being aimless and even useless.

Every sermon does not automatically need to have "three points and a poem." There must be a specific strategy to accomplish a specific purpose (mission). The strategy process might be seen in a typical visit to the doctor when someone is sick. First, the doctor examines the patient, then he offers a diagnosis of what the problem is (not just identifying the symptoms), then a prognosis for recovery is presented along with a prescription or treatment. In the same way, the preacher, through the sermon preached, may ask the listener to examine themselves in light of what Scripture says, then allow Scripture to make a diagnosis of what problems exist, then he presents the prognosis of hope that only God can give (or the consequence of ignoring the diagnosis), followed by a prescription from His word to achieve the desired result—spiritual health.

As part of the strategy, a preacher determines which sermon structure will best serve the mission of the sermon. Should it be topical, textual, "topogetical" (an exegetical sermon presented as topical in format), biographical, geographical? The length of the sermon will be determined by the mission to be accomplished. If 45 minutes are required to accomplish the mission of this sermon, then he won't go a minute less. But if it only takes 28 minutes to accomplish the purpose, he won't go a minute more. Be aware: it changes with every sermon, because every sermon's mission is different.

A sermon's strategy must take into consideration the listener and their learning style. There are many ways in which listeners learn. Some listeners are analytical, visual, or auditory. Any given sermon event may have a variety of these or even some other type(s) of learners present. The preacher must decide if the sermon is directed primarily to non-Christians, families, singles, men, women, etc. Although a sermon may be presented to a general or mixed set of listeners, strategy demands that the preacher consider all the possibilities and develop the sermon appropriately. Better sermon strategy preparation considers all the characteristics of the listeners.

The overall mission of a sermon determines not only the strategy, but also the structure to be used. Strategy can be seen in the organized structure of the sermon, especially the outline. The outline is the sermon's framework. It is essential for a well-built sermon. It serves as a tool to organize the sermon and its individual components. The outline gives form to the sermon. It lends support and stability to the sermon. The outline insures *balance* in the sermon (each part is given equal attention). The outline insures *unity* in the sermon (all parts tie to the overall purpose of the sermon). It insures *harmony* in the sermon (each part works with each other part). It insures *progression* in the sermon (each part moves the sermon forward). The outline is the framework that insures the sermon accomplished the predetermined purpose. For example, a builder determines the kind of framework structure to be used in light of the purpose of the building being built. A skyscraper has a different framework than does a doghouse. The sermon framework, made up of main and sub points, definitions, illustrations and the like, will be constructed on the foundation of spiritual truth. And everything in the sermon will hang on that structure. A quality structure (outline) has additional value to the preacher for his organization and memorization and for the listener as they understand, process, and accept the teaching.

There are several essential structural elements to every sermon: the Introduction, Body, and Conclusion. These serve as a framework of the sermon. They each have a specific function in the structure of the sermon, and each tie directly to the mission to be accomplished. The parts of the sermon, and their arrangement, are determined by the objective to be accomplished.

The Introduction

I recently took a cruise. The travel agent sent me a full-color travel brochure to tell me all about the trip, the route we would take, the stops we would make, and the things that we would see. Not only did it inform me; it excited me about the trip that lay ahead. After looking at the brochure, I could hardly wait to go on the trip. The Introduction is where the sermon begins (however, it is the last element to be written). It serves the strategy like a travel brochure, previewing and showing the highlights of the trip ahead. It invites and entices the listener to go on the sermon trip. It's a promise to be kept. It is where you grab the listener's attention.

The heart of the Introduction is showing the relevance of the sermon's message to the listener and their real-life situations. Few will follow if they don't understand the value of the message to their life. Showing this relevance early is primary to a successful sermon. Relevance is not found in contemporary language or the latest technology. Relevance is in the usefulness of God's truth to everyday life. Effective Introductions grab the listener's attention, preview the sermon, and show the relevance of the sermon to real-life situations.

The Body

When a golfer plays a round of golf, he has as his objective, one thing: getting the ball into the cup. From club selection to club selection, stroke by stroke, from tee to green he moves towards his goal. A beautiful long drive is worth nothing if his putting misses the mark. Any golfer knows, "You drive for show, but you putt for dough." The Body of the sermon is the fairway for the preacher. Each point and sub-point are the clubs he selects to move the truth of God's Word closer and closer to its destination—the heart of the listener. During the sermon "round," he explains, clarifies, defines, demonstrates, proves, illustrates, describes, and reasons. Whatever it takes to bring truth and heart together. He takes no unneeded strokes, nothing that leads him off course. Every part has a purpose. The body of the sermon is where the real "preaching" is done.

Transitions

Anyone who learns to drive a manual transmission remembers the first time they tried to coordinate shifting the stick-shift, operating the clutch, and accelerating at the same time. It was a rough time (especially for the neck of the one teaching us). Over time, however, we learned to make the transition between the gears smoothly without anyone hardly noticing. Moving from one element of the sermon requires smooth transitions as well for it to flow conversationally. It needs smooth transitions from the Introduction into the Body, from the Body into the Conclusion, from one main point to the next, in and out of illustrations, or reading of Scripture. This blending of the elements allows the sermon to move almost seamlessly from beginning to end. Often the elements of transition are constructed "on the fly" extemporaneously. A well-prepared preacher sees the value of these transitions and constructs them in advance, even to the extent that they are written word for word as part of the sermon body itself. Well-prepared transitions not only smooth from one point to point, but also serve as mini introductions and conclusions between those points, let the listeners "catch up" and process the points offered, and help to restate the overall purpose of the sermon.

Every part of the body serves the overall purpose of the sermon. However, be careful not to be so concerned with the "wheelbarrow" of structure that you forget the load it carries (message).

The Conclusion

When I was a boy, I begged my father to buy one of those gigantic "4th of July Celebration" packs of fireworks. We played with the foaming charcoal snakes, the sparklers, then we moved from the small fireworks that hopped all around the ground, to the bottle rockets to the roman candles and then to the finale, the big "Statue of Liberty" that emits sparks and played the national anthem. It was moved to the center of our street. Neighbors paused to see the spectacular. My father was called upon to light the fuse. Then...psssssssss...pfith...and it was done. It was disappointingly anti-climatic.

The Conclusion is the climax of the sermon, and as such, it should be a powerful crescendo to the sermon preached. Sometimes sermons begin with great promise and enthusiasm, only to fizzle in the end. The conclusion is where the sermon ends, where it is reviewed and, most importantly it is where it is applied. If the Conclusion is too short, it's like turning the nose of a plane straight down to land it—disaster. If the Conclusion is too long, it will "miss the runway" all together—equally a disaster. The sermon reached its altitude gradually, point by point. The Conclusion must reverse the process in miniature to bring the listener back to where the sermon trip started. It brings the sermon back to the promise that was made in the Introduction, back to the relevance for those who have taken the trip. The conclusion isn't just the end of the sermon, it should answer the "So why does any of this matter?" question.

Make Application

At the center of the Conclusion is the application of the truth taught. It is a call to action that is the natural and obvious extension of the sermon preached. It should include not only the "what we must do," but also the how-to do it.

The application should be:

1. Personal: It needs to be directed at individuals, not by name, but certainly by situations. The listeners should understand that the message is for *them*, not someone else.
2. Present Tense: It needs to include something that they should do, starting *now*.
3. Dynamic. It needs to have a motivational aspect that, using proper emotion, encourages the

listener to take *action*.
4. Practical and Purposeful. It needs to be something that meets a *real-life* situation.
5. Attainable. It needs to be something that they reasonably *can* do—baby steps toward the ultimate goal.
6. Specific. It needs to be *clear* in its instruction.

The application is not manipulation, forcing action (we are not salesmen). The application is motivating action, change, or obedience by bringing the insight of God's word.

The application is traditionally offered in the form of an invitation. It is an invitation to apply the message preached to one's individual situation. As such, this invitation must be consistent with the truth that has been expounded upon. An invitation to "obey the Gospel," as part of a sermon on what it takes to be a godly spouse, would be inconsistent and ineffective. An invitation to be more evangelistic when the sermon was a call to become a child of God through baptism would also be a poor use of the application. The application (invitation) *must always* be consistent with the message preached.

Now the sermon is complete, but the preparation is not. It is now time to prepare to present the material. Time now needs to be spent reviewing, reflecting, and revising the sermon. Time needs to be spent becoming intimately familiar with it. Practicing it over and over in your head, and even out loud to make it as perfect as it can be. Preparation is not complete until the preacher is fully prepared to preach the sermon that he has prepared.

It is estimated that preparation can alleviate as much as 75% of stage fright. That may or not be true if even measurable, but one thing is certain—preparation is essential to effective preaching. The better the preparation, the better the preacher.

The better the preparation, the better the sermon. The better the preparation, the better the presentation. The better the preparation, the better the results. And that's not just better, that's best!

9

better attitude
trey morgan

Preaching is a wonderful thing when done well. Climbing into the pulpit with what you believe is a good sermon doesn't always mean it will turn out as well as you expect, but giving a sermon with the right attitude makes all the difference.

When my youngest son, Cooper, was five, he revealed to me something that I did not know about him. On our ride home from church, he looked up at me with all seriousness and said, "Dad, I'm sorry, but I just don't like church."

I was floored, shocked, and had I not been a preacher, I would've been speechless. So I kindly and calmly asked him, "Son, what is it about church that you don't like?" I could see him take a deep breath, and not wanting to make eye contact with me, he said, "The preaching, Dad, I don't like the preaching. It's just too long." At that point, I calmly pulled the car to the side of the road, opened the door, and told the little fella, "Get out!"

Just kidding.

But honestly, what was I to say to my five-year-old son? I smiled at Cooper to let him know it was going to be okay. His questioning blue eyes that were now looking at me told me that he was waiting for some kind of response to his statement. I finally leaned over and told him the truth. "Son," I said, "Sometimes I don't like the preaching either." He looked a little surprised and said, "Really, Dad?" I said, "Yes sir." And then at that point, I did my best to explain to a five-year-old boy that God loves him very much, and that I still love him very much as well. I told him that as he grows bigger and learns more about the Bible, that preaching won't be as boring, and he might actually like it. I'm not real sure he believed that last statement.

I too remember when I was a kid, thinking many times while sitting in a church pew, "How much longer is the sermon going to be?" A long sermon when I was a kid wasn't measured by time, but whether I could relate to it. Sometimes a ten-minute sermon seemed like an eternity, and other times a thirty-minute sermon seemed really short. I clearly remember as a young boy many sermons that were preached in such a good way that it had a lasting effect on me.

I have often wondered what made, and still makes, the difference between sermons that I considered to be good and sermons that I wanted to end as soon as possible? If I can vividly remember sermons from my childhood and teen years that touched me, obviously there was something about them that were different than the ones that I wanted to end quickly. Even today as a 48-year-old man who has been preaching for over 25 years, I am still a student of good gospel messages and good sermons. I will be the first to admit that there is a difference between a sermon that you would like to end quickly and a good sermon that really challenges you. I've come to realize that most all of the sermons that I've ever considered good had a key ingredient in those sermons that was the right attitude.

Yes, attitude. The right attitude isn't just important while preaching; it is essential.

There are many components that make up an attitude in preaching. I'm not talking about, "Did you get a good night of sleep?" or "Has everyone been nice to you this week?" What I am saying is this: Your attitude will be based on whether you see what you do as a preacher as eternally important or just a job. Having the opportunity to stand before a group of people and talk about Jesus is a great privilege and honor. It is something that you should be passionate about. Without passion and without seeing it as a privilege, it becomes just a job or duty, and it should never be that. When preaching becomes "just a job" to you, it is time for serious attitude change or possibly a career change. No one ever said that being a minister or preacher would be without troubles, trials, or struggles, but you still can continue with the attitude that you are blessed to do what you do.

"Have this mind among yourselves, which is yours in Christ Jesus," is what Paul said in Phil. 2:5. Paul said that Jesus' attitude was one in which he put others' needs above his own, he didn't see his coming to this earth as a job or a duty, but as an honor to do the will of His Father. It was done out of love for us.

I want to share with you five words that are essential ingredients to of a preacher's attitude.

passion

An attitude of passion is essential in preaching. Jesus was passionate about doing the will of the Father, which was coming to this earth to save man. He was passionate about sharing God's words with the world. In the same way, passion for preaching, for people, and for Jesus is something every minister needs. If you are in ministry, and especially if you teach/preach, then what you get to do is an honor. It is not a job or a duty, but a privilege. It's a very special privilege that not all people can or get to do. The passion that you have for ministry, people and preaching is not something that happens by accident—you seek it. You seek passion by continually seeking a relationship with God. Having the right attitude and passion will make an amazing difference in your preaching. People will want what you're sharing.

Years ago, my brother-in-law started selling kitchen knives part-time to help supplement his income. I got the dreaded phone call saying he wanted to come over and talk to us. I figured that he was going to try to sell us his knives. I believe my exact phrase to my wife was, "He can come talk to us until he's blue in the face, but we don't need any of his dumb kitchen knives." I remember thinking, "He can come tell us all about those knives, but I refuse to buy any."

When my brother-in-law left my house that night, I was the new owner of a set of kitchen knives. Yes, I was impressed with the demonstrations of the knives, but I was more sold on how passionate he was about them. He believed in them, in what he was selling, and I honestly believed that he wanted me to own a set of knives—not because he needed the money, but because my kitchen needed the knives. I remember thinking to myself, "How could I not have a set of these knives in my kitchen?" His passion for what he was doing oozed out of him. He believed in his product, and he wanted to help make my wife's job easier by providing her with the right tools in the kitchen to get it done. Was he a good salesman? Yes, but he was also very passionate about what he was sharing, and that made the real difference.

It is essential that we are passionate and remain passionate about what we are sharing with others. Don't let Satan, others, or busy-ness snuff out your passion. Passion for the Gospel, for preaching, and for Jesus never happens by accident. It takes deliberate pursuit. Our attitude is directly affected by the passion in our lives for what we do. Sadly, when we begin to see preaching as just something we do, we lose that passion.

Jesus was always passionate about the words he shared with others. It was because they are life-changing words and words that affect people's eternal destiny. Don't ever take lightly what you do. You are a spokesman for God. If you are privileged and honored enough to stand before a congregation and deliver a message about the gospel of Jesus, it is imperative that you have the right attitude and be passionate about what you're saying.

I love being a minister. I love getting to be a part of people's lives at their biggest events—births, baptisms, weddings, funerals, etc. I love helping people and watching them grow spiritually. But right up at the top of the list of things I love about being a minister is the honor and responsibility of preaching the good news. I love preaching. I always have. Nothing is more exciting to me than getting to stand up in front of people and talk about our Father and His amazing Son. Preaching is what I'm passionate about, and if the day ever comes that I don't feel that way anymore, I probably need to find something else to do.

humility

Another way in which you can have the right attitude in preaching is realizing that what you're doing is not about you. Another essential ingredient to preaching with the right attitude is humility. Humility is often a tough thing for the preacher because, while preaching, you are the center of attention. When I hear things like, "You're such a good speaker," or "I love the way you communicate to us," I have to remember to be cautious that my preaching doesn't start becoming about me. Instead, I must keep it focused on Christ. You and I are just instruments being used by God to do his work.

Pride makes it easy to want to become the center of attention. Too many good preachers have been taken down by pride. When we make it about ourselves, when we're unable to take constructive criticism, or when we become narcissistic, it is unhealthy for both the preacher and the listeners. Yes, we are the ones doing the speaking and the spotlight seems to be on us, but do not allow your sermon to become about you. Our mission is to proclaim the good news to people and point them towards Jesus—not towards preachers, committees or even churches. Back in the same text we looked at earlier in Phil. 2—

> Have this mind among yourselves, which is yours in Christ Jesus, who, though he was in the form of God, did not count equality with God a thing to be grasped, but emptied himself, by taking the form of a servant, being born in the likeness of men. And being found in human form, he humbled himself by becoming obedient to the point of death, even death on a cross. Therefore God has highly exalted him and bestowed on him the name that is above every name, so that at the name of Jesus every knee should bow, in heaven and on earth and under the earth, and every tongue confess that Jesus Christ is Lord, to the glory of God the Father.

We're told that Jesus "humbled himself." The whole text is about the fact that Jesus wasn't concerned about his position with being God. It was about giving up everything to redeem man back to God. Preaching isn't about praise for ourselves; it's about us getting out of the way to point others towards Jesus.

Maybe my favorite part of Phil. 2 is the part where Jesus humbles himself and makes himself a servant. Humble people are servants. It's hard to be prideful while washing someone's feet, mowing someone's lawn, or cleaning out a church van. Want a good gauge on your pride as a man of God? Ask yourself how willing are you to be first in line to serve others. One of the scariest scriptures in God's word is found in Jas. 4:6, where it says, "God opposes the proud, but gives grace to the humble." We should never insist on everything being our way or for our glory, or God will work against us. If you crave glory, recognition, and attention, then something is not right.

I believe it was pride that caused Satan to rebel against God. It was pride that caused Adam and Eve to eat the forbidden fruit because they wanted to be like God. It is pride that takes out many a good preacher who starts making his ministry and his preaching about himself.

simplicity

Make it your goal each week to strive to get across a point that will be clearly seen. Talk about things of relevance needed in people's lives. When they leave, they should feel challenged. If they don't, you've missed your opportunity. Our goal as God's spokesman is to share the message in such a way that everyone gets it—young and old, educated and uneducated.

There often seems to be two kinds of teachers in this world: communicators and intellectuals. Communicators can take the difficult-to-understand and make it simple, while intellectuals take the simple-to-understand and make it difficult.

Unfortunately in the world of preaching, sometimes there are far too many intellectuals trying to communicate the gospel today in a way that is difficult for people to understand. Dig, study, and present the milk and meat of God's word, but do it in a way that people clearly understand, using topics that are relevant in people's lives.

Jesus was a communicator who spoke clearly about subjects that were relevant to people's life. Jesus taught about significant things that people needed to know. Things like eternity, death, how to treat one another, how to forgive, and how to enter the kingdom of God. He covered topics like adultery, anger, worry, debt, doubt, faith, giving, greed, honesty, hypocrisy, joy, kindness, lust, marriage, money, parenthood, prayer, sex, giving, taxes, trust, and many other things. People were able to apply what Jesus was teaching. He didn't just tell people what was wrong, but he told them how to fix things. I love the fact that you could apply what Jesus taught. People who heard Jesus speak felt challenged when Jesus finished preaching. Our goal should be always to present the gospel in such a way that it's clear, understandable, and applicable. Preach like Jesus. Jesus knew then what we are just figuring out—people remember things like stories and pictures. Jesus painted pictures with his words that left people remembering what he had taught.

A few years ago, I ran into a lady whose church had hired a new preacher. She said, "I just love him to death. He preaches just like Jesus." I asked inquisitively, "Really, how is that?" She said, "He doesn't tell any of those stories and just quotes lots of Scripture in his sermons." As I was standing there debating in my head whether to pop this lady's bubble about how Jesus really preached, someone else walked up, and I didn't get a chance to tell her that she had it all backwards. When you read through the Gospels, you find Jesus quoting very few Scriptures. Instead, you find him constantly telling people stories that applied to their lives. While I'm not advocating in any form removing God's Word from our sermons, I am saying that Jesus obviously knew how to reach people, and we can learn from him. Jesus communicated with stories, parables, and painted word-pictures to get across his point. He was the master storyteller. He made points with things like a towel, a bird, a fish, a tree, a flower, a coin, a sheep, a child, a plank, etc. to make a point. There was nothing dull about Jesus' lessons.

We need deep biblical teaching and preaching, but understand this: The deep teaching we need is what will make a difference in people's day-to-day lives. As D.L. Moody once said, "The Bible was not given to increase our knowledge but to change our lives. The goal is Christ-like character."

When it comes to God's Word and simplicity, there is nothing boring about them. When people understand a sermon, they get more out of it. It has always bothered me when I heard people say, "Church (or preaching) is boring." I personally think the only place where there should be boring churches or preaching is in Boring, Oregon (yes, an actual place), where I've found with the help of Google Maps that there are actually 25 Boring churches. May God forgive us when we take the most exciting book in the world and make it dull.

positivity

Positive preaching is such a hot topic these days because there are men who claim to speak God's Word, but have simply changed God's message into motivational "feel-good" pep-rallies. My fear is that because people have swung the pendulum of the clock too far one way, often times our natural response is to swing it back too far the other way. What we need is a healthy balance in the pulpit and in our preaching, but our goal for every sermon remains the same—encourage the body. Encouraging the body comes when we have the attitude that our sermons aren't just about pointing out what we're doing wrong, but also about building others up.

"Let no corrupting talk come out of your mouths, but only such as is good for building up, as fits the occasion, that it may give grace to those who hear" (Eph. 4:29). Paul reminds us that Christians are to "build others up" according to their needs. There is hope in that, and people need to hear hope. People need a message that is full of hope. A message that builds up, not just tears down.

My mother grew up listening to preaching every Sunday, and I always valued her godly wisdom. I asked her once about the preacher she had where she attended church. I'll never forget her words when she said, "He's a good man, but we've not done anything right in his eyes since he's been here." I asked her what exactly she meant and she said, "For the past three years all we've heard are sermons about what we're doing wrong. Not once have we heard how to fix it or that it can even be fixed." She sighed and continued, "He doesn't give much hope for anyone." It hurt my heart to hear my godly mother say that. Preaching should be about giving hope, finding answers, and showing people the way—not about beating people down. Our sermons should be oozing with love that is pointing people to a merciful and gracious God. Our God is not a heavenly policeman waiting to catch someone doing wrong so that he can write him a spiritual ticket. Our God is our loving Father who loved us enough to allow His only Son to die for us.

One of the greatest encouragers in my life is my friend Mike. He is a godly man who shepherds the church where I preach.

Dr. Mike works out in the world and sees people at their worst. Mike has quoted a phrase to me so many times about preaching that has become my personal mantra in preaching. If Mike has told me once, he's told me a thousand times, just before I get up to speak, "Give them heaven today." I will never forget that. It's Mike's way of reminding me that people have been through enough hell this week already. What they need from me is a little heaven … a little hope. Hope! They need to hear that there is hope. Hope that there is more to this world than bills, struggles, marriage problems, trials and temptations. "Give them heaven," my friend Mike says. It is something I try to do every Sunday.

longevity

Finally, I really want you to catch the word *longevity*. It's important that you last in ministry. You need to have an attitude that says, "I need to take care of myself physically, emotionally and spiritually so that I do not burn out or disqualify myself from what I'm honored to do." We need good men preaching the gospel, and too many of them are getting out. Sure, there will be tough times, but hopefully there will be many more rewarding days than hard days.

I still remember my first real sermon that I preached when I was a teenager. I had known all my life that I wanted to be a preacher, and this sermon was going to be the start of what I hoped would be a life-long career. My first sermon was on a Sunday night in a small country church. They'd asked me to fill in that night while their preacher was gone, and this teenager was nervous about it. I'd done a couple of short Wednesday night devotionals but never a real Sunday sermon.

I remember that night vividly. I can remember my topic and

even the points of my sermon. I still remember the song I decided to lead during the sermon that went along with the topic of my lesson. What I remember most was that none of it went well. In fact, it was pretty much a nightmare. I was so nervous I could barely talk. It just so happened that the song I chose to lead, *no* one in the entire church knew it. So I pretty much did a solo during the whole song, which was pure terror to this teenage boy. The most painful thing that evening was knowing that those poor people had to sit through what I believe was probably the worst sermon ever.

As I stepped down from the pulpit following the sermon, I remember thinking, "I'll *never* do that again. I'm just not cut out for preaching." As customary, the preacher was to go to the back after the sermon and shake hands with everyone as they left. I took the long dreaded walk of shame from the front to the back. I didn't want to talk to anyone, and I prayed that the Lord would just come back right then and take us all to heaven.

While walking to the back, I looked up, and there stood my dad. He'd driven an hour to come hear me preach my first sermon. I gave him a half smile, ducked my head, and took my place by the door to shake hands with everyone as they left. As people walked by, I got more than a few tips on things I could do better, but most people were nice enough just to smile and walk on by. Then my dad walked up. He stuck out his hand and shook mine, then smiled and said, "Son, that was a great sermon." Then he added, "Whatever you do, don't ever stop preaching."

Twenty-five years later, I'm thankful for two things. I'm thankful that God put my dad there that night when I preached that horrible sermon. And I'm thankful that I took my dad's advice and didn't quit. May you always have the right attitude, the attitude of Jesus … and may you never stop preaching.

10

better prayer life
adam faughn

"How ironic," I thought.

I had just been thinking in previous days about how I needed to spend more time in serious, fervent prayer, and my phone rang, asking me to write a chapter for a book for preachers on how to have a better prayer life. The words to the classic hymn, "God Moves in a Mysterious Way," echoed around my mind a few times, as you might imagine.

There is a common problem with how preachers conclude sermons. Too many of us can turn the "application" portion of the sermon—any sermon—into just two things: (1) read the Bible more, and (2) pray more. It does not matter what we are preaching about; some of us end with those two takeaways nearly every Sunday.

Certainly, those things are true, but may I ask: how are we actually doing in following our own constant advice? I do not think we should end every sermon with those being the only takeaways, but maybe some of us need to reexamine those sermons and then look into our own lives and see if we are as dedicated to those two things as we ask those who listen to us week in and week out to be.

We know, and I'm sure we have all preached, that God does not require us to pray a certain number of times each day or to recite some rote, mindless chant that qualifies as a prayer. We all have reminded our listeners on multiple occasions of the short but powerful words of 1 Thess. 5:17, "Pray without ceasing." And we have probably made the requisite joke about not having to close our eyes while praying behind the wheel of a car.

As a preacher, though, are we not in constant communication with the Lord already? I mean, we spend hours every week digging into the Word and trying to mine truths that will change hearts and lives for eternity. We read our Bible at least daily, and probably spend a large chunk of our week in just a handful of verses. We are, as we say, "hearing from the Lord" through His Word regularly and constantly.

But are we praying to Him?

In this chapter, I want to remind us all of things we have regularly preached. But I want us to forget about preparing these things to outline in a sermon, and instead I want us to open our own hearts and lives and see if we have been practicing what we preach when it comes to prayer.

pray constantly

This is where 1 Thess. 5:17 comes into play, but so do many more biblical principles. "Pray without ceasing" is a good place to start, but we have all preached that the idea is to pray in any and every circumstance.

Preachers, are we only praying to God in a few circumstances? Maybe we only pray when we have had a busy week and need to "get up" a quick sermon before Sunday comes. Maybe we only pray when we are spouting a few accomplishments to heaven (how many have been baptized during this meeting, for example).

Instead, we should be praying in every circumstance. If you want to preach better, pray throughout the week. Pray for wisdom as you consider what to preach, both short- and long-term. Pray for wisdom as you study each text or topic. Pray for more wisdom when you feel stuck in your understanding. Pray for encouragement when your motivation is waning. Pray for focus when you are tempted not to do all the good you can do. Pray for forgiveness when you sin. Pray for balance in your life.

We often teach that a person does not have to pray at any certain time of the day, but that prayer is constant communication with the Lord, and that line of communication never closes. Do we treat it that way? Too often, it is easy to get so caught up in the work of ministry that we forget to check off what should be priority number one: talking to the Lord.

Jesus arose early in the morning to pray, prayed all night on more than one occasion, and had many other prayers that are recorded for us. As busy as our Lord was, prayer was constantly the first priority in His life. You and I are not too busy to pray at various times throughout our day.

pray fervently

I cannot speak for every person who will read these words, but I want to share something with you. I regularly struggle to pray with deep emotion. Probably because I am male, I keep so many things in my life on an intellectual level and remove a lot of the emotion from them. Too often, that emotionless way of doing things infiltrates my prayer life.

James famously wrote, "The effectual fervent prayer of a righteous man availeth much" (Jas. 5:16 KJV). That is about the only time I ever use the word "fervent," but it is a powerful word. In fact, it is the Greek term from which we get our English word "energy." Our prayers need to have an energy about them.

This is not just talking about the prayers we might lead in public, either. Each prayer we utter to the Lord needs to have energy and emotion. It is not difficult to fill a prayer with energy when we are celebrating a great spiritual victory. But when we are down, discouraged, or tempted, we can try to get by with nothing more than a rote prayer, filled with very few real feelings behind it.

If you are struggling in your work, let your heart and mind meet in prayer. If you are struggling with a text or how to present a difficult truth to the congregation, do not keep things on an unfeeling, dispassionate level. Take that difficulty before God's throne and pour it out before Him.

It is important for us to remember that the shortest verse in the Bible, "Jesus wept" (John 11:35), sits just a few verses before Jesus lifts up both His heart and His motive before the throne of God in prayer (vv. 41-42). There is very little that is "intellectual" about this brief prayer; it is almost all emotion and motivation.

Your prayers do not have to be long, but they need to combine both your mind and your heart. If you want to preach as well as you can, take it all before God's throne where you will find help.

pray humbly

Oh, how I wish I didn't need to include this point when writing to preachers! But the very words of our Lord make it clear that we all need this reminder.

In Luke 18:9-14, Jesus told the parable of the two men who went to the temple to pray. The one we often focus on is the one called a sinner, who said a short prayer, asking for God's mercy. We focus on him simply because he turns out to be the real example of the type of penitent heart the Lord desires for us to have. However, I want to focus on the Pharisee in Jesus' story for a moment. If I am not careful, my prayers can sound a bit too much like his.

The prayer of this Pharisee is a list of accomplishments. "God, I thank you that I am not like other men, extortioners, unjust, adulterers, or even like this tax collector. I fast twice a week; I give tithes of all that I get" (vv. 11-12). I doubt any of us have ever used these words as our "model prayer," but does the hollow arrogance behind them strike us as something we might be guilty of at times?

It is far easier to pray our accomplishments to the Lord than to pray our faults and needs. When we are like the other man in Jesus' parable, we must simply admit that we are sinners and need mercy. Frankly, I hate admitting that! I would much rather let God know how good He has it to have me in the pulpit and helping people throughout the week. I would rather make sure God remembers the percentage I give on Sunday and how many of my hours are spent in His service. The problem is simply that this is not praying; that's résumé writing!

Preachers, I have no doubt, are among the very best people in the world. I enjoy spending time with those who know the ins and outs of the life of ministry, and I am constantly amazed at the faithfulness of so many who are true to the Lord in their life of service. However, if we are not careful, we can let that go to our heads, and it can even infiltrate our prayer life.

First, we will cease—or at least lessen—prayer. After all, we are too busy doing the good we are supposed to be doing. The Lord needs me on the front lines, so why should I stop to pray!?

But even beyond that, when we do stop to pray, is it nothing more than a list of what we have done for God? Or is there humility in our prayers? Is there an amazement that God could possibly use a jar of clay such as me to do anything that is to His glory in this world? When we stop to consider what we are doing in this world, it should not fill us with pride; it should fill us with amazement of the Almighty.

Consider again Jesus' prayer before raising Lazarus. While some of the words were about Himself, the focus was on the Father. "So they took away the stone. And Jesus lifted up his eyes and said, "Father, I thank you that you have heard me. I knew that you always hear me, but I said this on account of the people standing around, that they may believe that you sent me" (John 11:41-42).

If someone were able to read your mind in your private prayers, would that person think you were focused on yourself, or seeking to glorify the Lord in all you do? Pray with humility.

pray fully

Include things other than the Sunday sermon in your prayer life. Pray for and about many people, both near and far.

If you are married and/or have children, these precious souls need to be in your prayers constantly. While you may be "doing the work," they are a vital part of all you do and need your prayers for faithfulness and strength. They need you to pray that you will be the kind of husband/father they need.

Pray for your elders, even if you might be going through a time of strain with them. They bear a tremendous burden, and you need to pray for their wisdom and for your cooperative spirit.

Pray for various members of the congregation. The sick, the hurting, those you have counseled, the erring, those going through a time of transition, the depressed—all these need regular prayer. When you take those situations regularly before God's throne, it will help you be more in tune with how you can minister to them, both in the pulpit and out.

Pray for fellow preachers, both near and far. You may not know each one's specific situation, but you know the joys and the trials of ministry. If you know a specific need, pray! If you don't, pray for preachers in general, that they will stay true to the ways and the Word of God.

Each of us could add to that list, but this is a good place to start. Pray for as many different things as you can. If you must, keep an actual list to help you remember. If you prefer, simply pray for needs as they are put before you. Whatever your method, pray with others in mind, as well as yourself.

conclusion

Prayer should be as natural to the Christian as eating and breathing. Too often, we guilt trip people with our sermons by ending every one of them with the application to read and pray more. For some of us, though, it would be worth the time to ask: "Am I following my own advice?"

Without doubt, Jesus is the greatest preacher who ever lived. He was, and is, peerless. We can study His methods and read countless books and articles that show us exactly how He presented the truth to His hearers. One thing that is often missing in these analyses, though, is the clear point made throughout the Gospel accounts: Jesus spent time in prayer. His life and ministry were bathed in prayer, and there can be no doubt that was a huge part of what made Him peerless.

Paul was the greatest missionary the Lord's Church has ever known. While Paul had plenty of helpers along the way, he stands head and shoulders above anyone else who has ever tried to spread the Gospel to large portions of the world. Again, countless books and articles have been written showing Paul's speaking and writing styles, and how he could make a defense or an argument. Near the beginning and end of nearly every letter we have of Paul's, however, there is the constant theme of prayer. He prayed for himself but he also prayed for specific people, congregations, and situations. There is little wonder he was as remarkable as he was.

None of us will ever be Jesus, and none of us will have the worldwide impact Paul had. But can we not learn from their example? If I want to impact the lives of my family, the congregation where I serve, and the community in which I live (and even beyond), the only way I can do that is to be a man of prayer. There is still much work to be done, and the work begins, not in walking shoes or wingtips, but on praying knees. Only then will we preach and minister better.

about the authors

CHRIS MCCURLEY has been in ministry for 13 years. He currently serves as preaching minister for the Oldham Lane church of Christ in Abilene, TX. He is the husband of Libby and the father to Keely, Zoe, and Zane. He is an avid fan of the Dallas Cowboys, the St. Louis Cardinals, and relaxing in the mountains.

KEITH PARKER served as the pulpit minister for three different congregations for the first thirty years of his ministry; for the last six years, he has done full-time traveling evangelistic preaching for about fifty different congregations each year. He makes Hendersonville, TN his home whenever he is home. Keith and his wife, Sandra, have three children and two grandchildren. He loves Alabama football, travel, and spending time with family.

STEVE HIGGINBOTHAM has been preaching full-time for more than thirty years. He currently serves as the preaching minister at the Karns Church of Christ in Knoxville, TN and as an adjunct instructor in the Southeast Institute of Biblical Studies. He and his wife, Kim, have four children. Steve is a fan of the Pittsburgh Steelers and is a trivia enthusiast of *The Andy Griffith Show*.

CHUCK MONAN is the preaching minister for the Pleasant Valley Church of Christ in Little Rock, AR. He is a graduate of Oklahoma Christian University. Chuck is married to Susan, and they have two sons, Charlie and Nathan. He also moonlights as the Pigskin Preacher on 103.7 The Buzz.

MICHAEL WHITWORTH preaches for the Carter Lake Road Church of Christ in Bowie, TX and is the founder and owner of Start2Finish. He is the author of several books, including the award-winning *The Epic of God* and *The Derision of Heaven*. He loves the Dallas Cowboys, Alabama Crimson Tide, M&Ms, and drinking from large Mason jars. In his spare time, he enjoys reading, drinking coffee, watching sports, and spending time with his awesome family and furry golden retriever.

JAY LOCKHART has been preaching for over fifty years. He currently serves as the preaching minister and an elder of the Whitehouse, TX church of Christ. He is married to Arlene Carter Lockhart, and they have three grown children and six grandchildren. Jay is the author of *Truth For Today Commentary: Ephesians* and co-author (with Clarence DeLoach) of *The Glory of Preaching*.

JACOB HAWK serves as preaching minister for the Riverside Church of Christ in Kerrville, TX. He is the husband of Natalie and the father of Hayden and Hudson. Jacob also loves to write and has written three books: *Image of the Invisible God, The Hawk's Nest: 90 Lessons for Faith and Family,* and *When Mountains Won't Move: How to Survive a Struggling Faith.* When he's not preaching, writing, or spending time with family, Jacob is usually on the golf course.

WAYNE ROBERTS currently serves as the family and outreach minister for the Church of Christ in Ripon, CA. He and his wife, Tami, have been married since 1981 and conduct the *His Shoes, Her Shoes* marriage seminar. They have raised five grown children and are enjoying four grandchildren.

TREY MORGAN has been in ministry for 25 years. He currently serves as preaching minister for the Childress Church of Christ in Childress, TX. He is the husband of Lea and the father of four boys, Taylor, Parker, Connor, and Cooper. Trey loves short-term mission work in Honduras and is also actively involved in marriage ministry. He and his wife do weekend workshops for churches all over the U.S. called *Stronger Marriage Workshops.*

ADAM FAUGHN preaches for the 9th Avenue church of Christ in Haleyville, Alabama and has been a youth or pulpit minister for fifteen years. He is married to the former Leah Moon, and they are blessed with two children, Mary Carol and Turner. Adam loves reading, podcasts, and running his family blog at alegacyoffaith.us. He may or may not have a one-hit wonder playlist on Spotify.

acknowledgments

Thank you to my earthly family—Libby, Keely, Zoe, and Zane—for your love and support. I love you with every fiber of my being. You are a blessing beyond measure.

Thank you to my spiritual family—the Oldham Lane Church of Christ and the wonderful Christians I have had the privilege to meet in my travels as a minister. Your encouragement has strengthened me in my service to the Lord.

Thank you to my Creator, the Almighty God, and my Lord and Savior Jesus Christ. My heart is full of love and gratitude. I am in awe of your power and majesty. I will strive daily to give you my all.

— Chris McCurley

Made in United States
Orlando, FL
03 November 2021

10183234R00079